What Everyone Should Know About Credit Before Buying or Borrowing Again

by Ira U. Cobleigh and
the Editors of U.S.News & World Report Books

U.S.NEWS & WORLD REPORT BOOKS
A division of U.S.News & World Report, Inc.
WASHINGTON, D.C.

U.S.NEWS & WORLD REPORT BOOKS

Directing Editor: Joseph Newman

MONEY MANAGEMENT LIBRARY

Editor: Roslyn Grant

2300 N Street, N.W., Washington, D.C. 20037

First Printing, 1975
Second Printing, Revised, 1976
Third Printing, Revised, 1978

Trade Distribution by Simon & Schuster
New York, New York 10020

ISBN 0-89193-415-4
ISBN 0-89193-028-0 pbk.

Library of Congress Catalog Number 74-24989

Printed in the United States of America

Contents

Illustrations

Tables and Charts

Photograph

Acknowledgments

Ira U. Cobleigh and the Editors of *U.S.News & World Report Books* are grateful to the following for their assistance in gathering material for this book:

American Bankers Association, American Express Company, American Medical Association, American Petroleum Credit Association, American Telephone & Telegraph Company, Automobile Dealers Association, Bank of Commerce (New York), Bowery Savings Bank, Carl Byoir and Associates, Carte Blanche Corporation, Chrysler Financial Corporation, C.I.T. Financial Corporation, Credit Information Corporation of New York, Credit Union National Association, Diners Club, Education Research Foundation, Federal Housing Administration, Federal Reserve System, First National City Bank, Ford Motor Credit Company, General

Motors Acceptance Corporation, Gimbel Brothers, Guaranteed Student Loan Program, Household Finance Corporation, Institute of Life Insurance, Interbank Card Association (Master Charge), Paul Kaskel and Sons, Manufacturers Hanover Trust Company, Marine Midland Bank (New York), National Association of Mutual Savings Banks, National Association of Residents and Interns, National Consumer Finance Association, National Foundation for Consumer Credit, National Savings and Loan League, New York Stock Exchange, J.C. Penney Company, W.R. Simmons Company, Student Loan Marketing Association, The Tuition Plan, U.S. Department of Commerce, U.S. Department of Housing and Urban Development, United States League of Savings Associations, the Veterans Administration, and Visa USA, Inc.

Introduction

Over 105 million Americans borrow money regularly. This is not evidence of either poverty or chronic financial mismanagement. Rather, borrowing has become a way of life, enabling Americans to enjoy the good things months or years ahead of the time they could pay for them in cash.

Your credit-ability, then, can serve you well throughout your life, bringing you material things, services, and vacation trips—all comfortably budgeted out of income. For many families, borrowing has become a form of thrift whereby the regular monthly payments steadily build an ownership equity in a television set, a piano, an airconditioning unit, a car, or a house. Then, too, everyone faces an emergency once in a while, a crisis when money is the only answer—and borrowing is the only way to get it. Unemployment, an accident, a pile-up of unpaid bills, a serious illness—any of these may create a need for ready cash.

While credit can be a good thing, it can also be a dangerous thing. If you keep your installment or debt payments below a defined ceiling, you are likely to manage well. But tragedy can result from extravagant purchases and reckless spending habits which the availability of easy credit can encourage. When you are tempted to "keep up with the Joneses," you might bear in mind that the Joneses may be going broke themselves.

This book is intended to help the reader manage personal credit wisely—to secure money and goods at the best available terms, while observing the danger signals and avoiding the pitfalls which can bring disaster.

40% DOWN
8 MONTHS
TO PAY

CHAPTER 1

The History of Credit

When man was leading a primitive life in field, forest, or cave, or dwelling in a crude tent or shelter beside an ancient river, his financial problems were minimal. No money, no taxes, no mortgages or other debt, and no bank statement to decipher and verify each month. His needs were simple: deer or fish for the entrees; roots and grain to balance the diet.

As tribes and villages grew in population and man's skills advanced, his acquisitive nature began to assert itself. He wanted a club, an ax, a shovel, a pot, a goat, or a camel. If he did not possess these things he had three alternatives: he could take them by force (if he were strong enough) from a neighbor or a stranger; he could swap something in exchange; or he could borrow. If he were the friendly, peaceful type, he would try to borrow. From such a simple act as, say, the loan of a stone ax, we have, in the millennia since, created huge structures of debt owed not just by individuals and families, but by a broad aggregation of man-made institutions: religions, corporations, municipalities, states, and governments.

Three thousand years before the Christian era, a man in Sumeria named Arad-Sin lent sixteen crudely formed bars of silver to a man named Apil-Ilu-Shu. A stone tablet recorded the transaction, and was probably the first I.O.U. A peasant in the Greek city of Thebes in 198 B.C. left to posterity this early promissory note: "Further everything that I now possess or shall acquire is herewith pledged to Nokhutes until I shall have discharged my debt in full."

The first coins

The explosive expansion of debt and of borrowing, however, awaited the coining of money. Barter arrangements were complicated and awkward; and lenders sought, when paid off, to receive something of constant value. It was hard to figure whether you were getting a good deal if you lent a sheep and were repaid with ten shekels of grain.

About 560 B.C., King Croesus of Lydia, renowned for his great wealth, hit upon the idea of minting uniform coins of gold and silver. These coins were about the size of a lima bean and had a lion and a bear engraved on their face. Within a century the Persians adopted this coinage idea and minted a gold daric which circulated widely as currency in the commerce of the eastern Mediterranean world for over 200 years. Then, over the centuries, came a parade of coins: the Arab dinar, the Roman denarius and aureus, the Byzantine besant, Florentine florins, Venetian ducats, and so on down to the pound sterling, the franc, the mark, the yen, the guilder, and the dollar that serve as currency at the present time.

During the Middle Ages the goldsmiths who minted the coins, often for governments and rulers, conceived the idea of giving their receipts for gold in bar or coin instead of the actual gold units. These receipts were easier for traders to carry by land or sea and could be replaced if stolen or lost. Since only a few merchants or traders ever demanded the actual gold, represented by the receipt, the goldsmiths began issuing receipts in amounts greater than the gold in their possession. From being goldsmiths they became bankers, originating lending practices now in common use by commercial banks.

The goldsmiths' receipts led to another development in the history of money—and lending. Governments began to issue paper money, at first convertible into, or representing reserves of, gold and silver in their treasuries and later as fiat money, which became legal tender on the word of the government, without reference to any defined store of precious metal. The first paper money appeared in the eighteenth century.

With the invention and refinement of instantly negotiable money, it became possible to define debt in terms of a uniform unit, at once a measure of value, a medium of exchange, and a store of wealth. From then on, debts were not stated in amounts of goods but in money units of a given weight or fineness, or in paper monies defined as legal tender.

Famous borrowers

The custom of lending money caught on rapidly. The early Babylonians, Greeks, and Romans were prominent in extending credit; so were the Celts of Britain. The famous Code of Hammurabi (the Babylonian king and lawmaker), chiseled on stone about 2000 B.C., had provisions to prevent the poor debtor from being exploited by the rich. Later, in Athens, the renowned Solon decreed that it was not right for defaulting debtors to be sold into slavery. The rich and notoriously greedy Crassus in Roman times lent to Julius Caesar (a playboy as well as a general) 800 talents (about $2.5 million) mainly because he thought Caesar was a political comer. Crassus also lent large sums to two other prominent figures of the time, Mark Antony and Cicero. This credit enabled these gentlemen to acquire villas and farmlands, and obtained important political favors for Crassus. (He had the fire department concession in Rome and would not allow even a bucket of water to be thrown on a fire unless the anguished owner agreed to sell the blazing property to Crassus at a "fire sale" price.)

During the Middle Ages feudal lords, princes, kings, and cardinals borrowed money to throw costly parties, to maintain armies, to build castles, and to indulge other extravagant desires. All this required a great deal of money—much of it borrowed. Charles V became a Holy Roman emperor only after his supporters had borrowed the equivalent of a million dollars to buy the needed votes.

Not just rich, famous, and titled borrowers fill the pages of history. Tillers of the soil on the banks of the Euphrates, the Nile, or the Rhine faced emergencies that only instant money could solve. A drought or pestilence might ruin a crop so that the desperate peasant had to borrow to tide him over until the next harvest time, or sometimes the money was needed to buy seed for the next planting. The interest on such borrowing was often so burdensome that the peasant remained locked into debt for a lifetime.

The emerging moneylenders

To accommodate all these harried borrowers there developed, in each civilization, a small, canny, and durable group of moneylenders. In tribal, regional, or national aggregations of population there were always the spenders and the savers, with spenders forming the majority. As the savers amassed surpluses they became the investors—owners of property and livestock—and the moneylenders. A New Testament parable tells of a man rewarded for running one talent up to ten. He did it by lending money.

The goldsmiths of Europe became almost automatically the moneylenders, and great banking families arose among them: the Peruzzis and Bardis in Italy, the Fuggers in Germany, and the Rothschilds in Germany, Holland, France, and England. They had resources to extend large lines of credit to merchants and shippers (usually with pledge of cargo or ship as collateral), and to kings, the nobility, and the church, often protecting the loan by such collateral as gold, crown jewels, or a silver or copper mine. The moneylenders were generally looked down upon as usurers, but in some instances they were rewarded by grateful monarchs with titles of nobility. From these moneylenders, central banks, such as the Bank of England, evolved as the monetary and lending institutions of European nations.

The big contribution of modern times to the ever-growing use of credit was the invention of the installment purchase of goods.

Buy now, pay later

In 1850 an eccentric American mechanic named Isaac M. Singer joined forces with two other men to make sewing machines. Together they founded the Singer Sewing Machine Company. Their machine, representing a significant patented and technological breakthrough, had a price tag of $125, at a time when the average American family's annual income was about $525. Obviously, housewives could not afford these stitching machines if they had to pay cash. So Singer hit upon a plan for time payments, five dollars down and five dollars a month, which he launched in 1856. Within eighteen years the Singer Company had surged ahead, retailing more sewing machines than all of its American competitors combined, and setting the stage for marketing its products in Europe, India, China, Japan, and South America. Where payments in other lands were difficult to arrange because the natives moved about so frequently, Singer salesmen sought comakers or cosigners on time-payment contracts, even accepting fingerprints when the buyer or sponsor could not sign his name.

This novel selling method set in motion the most remarkable sales phenomenon of the nineteenth and twentieth centuries—the "hire purchase" plan, as it is still called in England, or "buy now, pay later" in the American idiom. Installment buying proved sound because per-capita incomes were rising and people kept up their payments on desirable and useful goods. Offering credit to the consumer generated more dynamic and global manufacturing and retailing of goods than could ever have been achieved by cash purchases. It was a prime reason for the explosive growth in the American economy with goods in great volume made and marketed annually, and acquired by monthly budget payments out of incomes of the purchasers, extending for as long as a three-year period.

While Singer has the honor of being the pioneer in consumer credit, this selling innovation never really flowered until after 1915. In that year Commercial Credit began financing time payments on Ford motor cars, when the delivered model sold for about $700 and the average industrial annual wage was about $635. Obviously a buyer in this income bracket, however eager, could not pay cash; but he could acquire a car by making

Debt Expansion in the U.S.

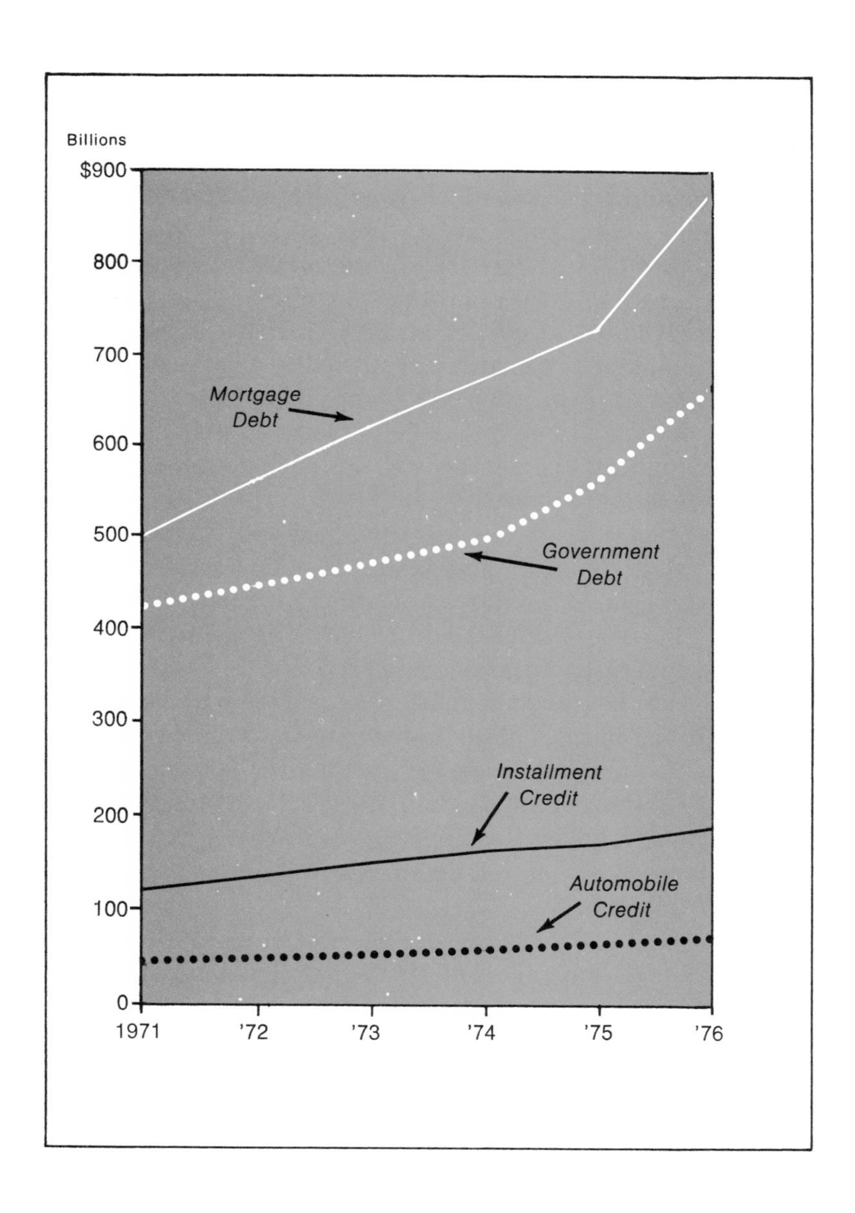

Source: *Federal Reserve Bulletin*

a modest down payment and complete the purchase by a series of monthly payments. Cash down in 1915 was about 40 percent, with the balance payable over the ensuing eight months. Since then down payments have been steadily lowered and the time periods extended, so that today thirty-six months' time for completion has become standard, and an increasing number of automobiles are now sold with nothing "down" and four years to pay. Over two-thirds of all new cars are marketed under installment contracts. Automobile debt ranks as the largest single category in the entire spectrum of consumer debt; and car installment credit is responsible for a significant percentage of the entire annual net profits of the auto industry.

While pioneered in sewing machines and maximized in car sales, "budget" purchasing is now standard retailing procedure for dozens of other products: household appliances, television sets, cameras, freezers, motor boats, campers, trailers, and mobile homes.

It is true that, in important measure, the high standard of living in the United States today and the vigor of our entire industrial economy are built upon massive extensions of credit. We would, in fact, have an instant depression if all current buyers of homes, furniture, cars, appliances, apparel, and pleasure boats had to pay cash on delivery.

This is not to say that either borrowing money or the acquisition of material comforts by extended payments is wrong, sinister, or dangerous. Rather the foregoing observations are designed to highlight: (1) the indispensability of credit in twentieth-century living; (2) the need of every individual to understand the vital place of credit in his financial planning; and (3) the position of interest charges and debt repayment as an almost continuous priority claim on earnings (about 17 percent of the average after-tax family income).

The importance of borrowing in the American economy is evident from the chart on page 21, which records indebtedness in the government, mortgage, and personal categories. This chart provides a graphic background for an understanding of the function of credit, its built-in contribution to the "good life," and the pitfalls, for individuals and the nation, if living beyond income and borrowing above capacity to repay become epidemic.

BANK OF

CHAPTER 2

Interest Rates—Usurious and Otherwise

The earliest borrowings were principally agricultural loans—advances to tide farmers or peasants over until their next crops were harvested. This type of credit extension is still prevalent in most of the world.

American farmers may borrow from banks in the spring to buy seed and fertilizer (and perhaps farm machinery), planning to pay back the loan in the fall, when the crops are brought in and sold. Peasants in other countries do the very same thing, but on a much smaller scale. In those lands there are millions of peasants who may carry a yoke of debt throughout their lives, or even lose ownership of their land, because a flood or drought destroys a planting and they lack the resources to pay off the principal, or even the interest that has been charged them, customarily at exorbitant rates.

Every business lending transaction involves two things: a stated principal amount—the sum borrowed and to be repaid in due course—and interest, which is the charge made for the use, or rental, of the money until the loan has been paid off.

No one knows when the first interest charge was made, but the custom was certainly flourishing in Babylonia around 2000 B.C. because Hammurabi's Code contained a rule to prevent the rich from gouging the poor, who borrowed from them.

Lending, even in early times, usually involved the pledging of something valuable to assure repayment—land, cattle, or even freedom. For centuries it was common practice for delinquent debtors to be sold into slavery. Later there were debtors' prisons, into which poor souls were cast if they could not pay their debts. Debt has ever led to human anguish, because the people most in need of loans have usually been on the lowest rung of the economic ladder with respect to resources and income, and possessed the least capability for repayment. In fact, without reference to settlement of principal, just trying to meet the interest payments has generally meant some kind of debtor thralldom for the poorest segment of the world's population.

The big difficulty has always been the interest rate—the price charged for the use of money. Historically this has been determined by the lenders because, in most instances, the borrowers were in no position to bargain. Their plight caused them to agree to pay the demanded rate or amount on the borrowed sum; otherwise, they did not get the money.

Moneylenders seen as villains

Those whose business it is to lend money to individuals today—banks, savings and loan associations, finance companies, and so forth—are respected and accepted institutions; but in most earlier centuries, the moneylender was cast as a villain, enjoying about the same social status as a modern gangster. This low opinion of moneylenders was the result of Biblical and early Christian moral codes, in which charging interest was cataloged as a sin and moneylenders were vilified as usurers who preyed on the people.

The Bible, in Deuteronomy, says: "Thou shalt not lend upon usury to thy brother; usury of money, usury of victuals or usury of anything that is lent upon usury." Later the reforms of Solon, in Athens, spelled out penalties for usury; so did the Justinian Code in Rome. The Christian Church carried on an aggressive crusade against usurers, with several specific papal encyclicals on the subject. Until the fourteenth century in Europe, usurers were subject to excommunication. In the Middle Ages persons of high standing avoided meeting moneylenders socially; and a good Christian was criticized if he sold a house to one.

The reason for all this downgrading of moneylenders was that many were, indeed, unscrupulous. The Shylocks of antiquity thought nothing of charging 40 to 100 percent annual interest. There must have been excellent international communication among them, because similar loan practices existed in Egypt, Mesopotamia, Rome, Spain, Britain, India, and China.

The moral indignation against, and religious condemnation of, usury lessened after the fourteenth century, because the Roman church had, itself, amassed a significant amount of wealth. During the Crusades, knights, lords, and barons, on their way to do battle in the Holy Land, often deposited their gold, jewels, or other treasure with the church (it was probably the safest place). Much of this wealth became the property of the church when Crusaders died or were captured or failed to return and claim their assets. Also some of the stored goods were specifically bequeathed to the church. In any event, the church became progressively richer; and like other individuals and institutions with funds for investment, it sought attractive returns. One of the best ways to glean this desired income was to lend money at interest. The church thus tempered its dislike for usury, and joined the ranks of the moneylenders. Later on, certain princes of the church became deeply involved financially and, in their need, turned to moneylenders, reluctantly accepting the high interest rates involved.

Behind all this concern about interest, there was always the question, "What is a usurious rate?" It was generally accepted by the fifteenth century that charging interest was at least partially justified. Money began to be understood as deserving of a rental, in the same way that farmland commanded an annual rental either in money or, more customarily, in a share of crops grown thereon. The problem of definition still remained, however. At what rate did rental of money become excessive, unfair, or confiscatory? Was 6 percent or 8 percent all right, and 25 percent or more usurious?

Simple annual interest

Properly speaking, simple interest is the annual interest rate or the amount paid for the use of money for a full year; and it is always stated in percentages. Variations in the time factor in the figuring of interest which have developed over the years have confused millions of people, who still think that all interest is charged as simple annual interest.

Those who have, since A.D. 1500, tried to regulate interest rates and to keep them reasonable have always used simple annual interest as the basis or yardstick. For over 500 years there have been specific laws against usury in Western nations and to regulate interest charges. Under Henry VIII, the legal interest rate in

England was restricted to 10 percent per annum; and a similar statute was passed during the reign of Elizabeth I. Then came some reductions—to 8 percent under James I; down to 6 percent under Charles II; and to 5 percent during the reign of Queen Anne (the lowest official rate recorded). George III passed a special law defining the legal rates on mortgages in Ireland or "in the colonies" (America) at no higher than 6 percent per annum.

Until 1969 the legal rate in most of our states was 6 percent per annum. By 1973, however, many states had been compelled to hike the legal rate to 8 or 8½ percent, because mortgage money, under inflationary economic conditions, was no longer available anywhere in the nation at as low a figure as 6 percent. Upward revision of the limit was essential to prevent the housing industry from entering a serious depression.

While legal rates (with the real estate mortgage market particularly in mind) became quite standardized, there grew up a series of other rates that affected business and banking practices, and led to considerable variations in charges, depending on the purpose and nature of the borrowing.

Fluctuation in rates

Since the founding of the Federal Reserve Banking System in 1913, we have developed a practical method for the regulation of interest rates in America under normal conditions. However, on several occasions (during both World Wars and after the Great Depression) the government itself has taken steps to control interest rates.

Under the Federal Reserve System, the basic rate has been the re-discount rate—the interest member banks would be required to pay on their own borrowings from the Federal Reserve Bank. That rate has ranged since

1913 from a low of ½ percent to a high of 8 percent in 1974.

Next of consequence is the prime rate—the percentage applying to loans made by commercial banks to their most credit-worthy corporate customers. This has varied quite sensitively in response to cyclical economic conditions; and reached a historical high of 12 percent in mid-1974.

Another influential quotation is for Treasury bills, the ninety-day obligations of the United States government. Interest rates on these securities were highly volatile in 1973-4, rising to 9½ percent. Also of interest is the yield on utility bonds rated AAA. The return on these bonds reached a low of 2.88 percent in 1947 and a high of 9 percent in April 1974. By March 1978 the yield had dropped to 8.45 percent.

Finally there is the yield on quality real estate mortgages. It was still around 8½ percent in April 1976. All of these charges have a bearing on the rate you will pay on a personal bank loan or a home mortgage or a time-purchase contract.

These rates, especially those for prime loans and Treasury bills, are market-sensitive and change frequently. All of them relate to loans of money (excluding those made by personal finance companies), and not to purchases of goods or services, which are covered in the chapters on installment merchandising.

Over and above these trends in the price of money, dictated by prevailing economic conditions in the private business sector, are the policies and decisions in the national interest made by the Treasury Department. During World War I there was a need for a policy to keep interest rates low so that the government might borrow on favorable terms; and citizens were urged—almost coerced—to prefer government bonds to other thrift or investment media. As the nation emerged from depres-

Short-Term and Long-Term Interest Rates in the U.S.

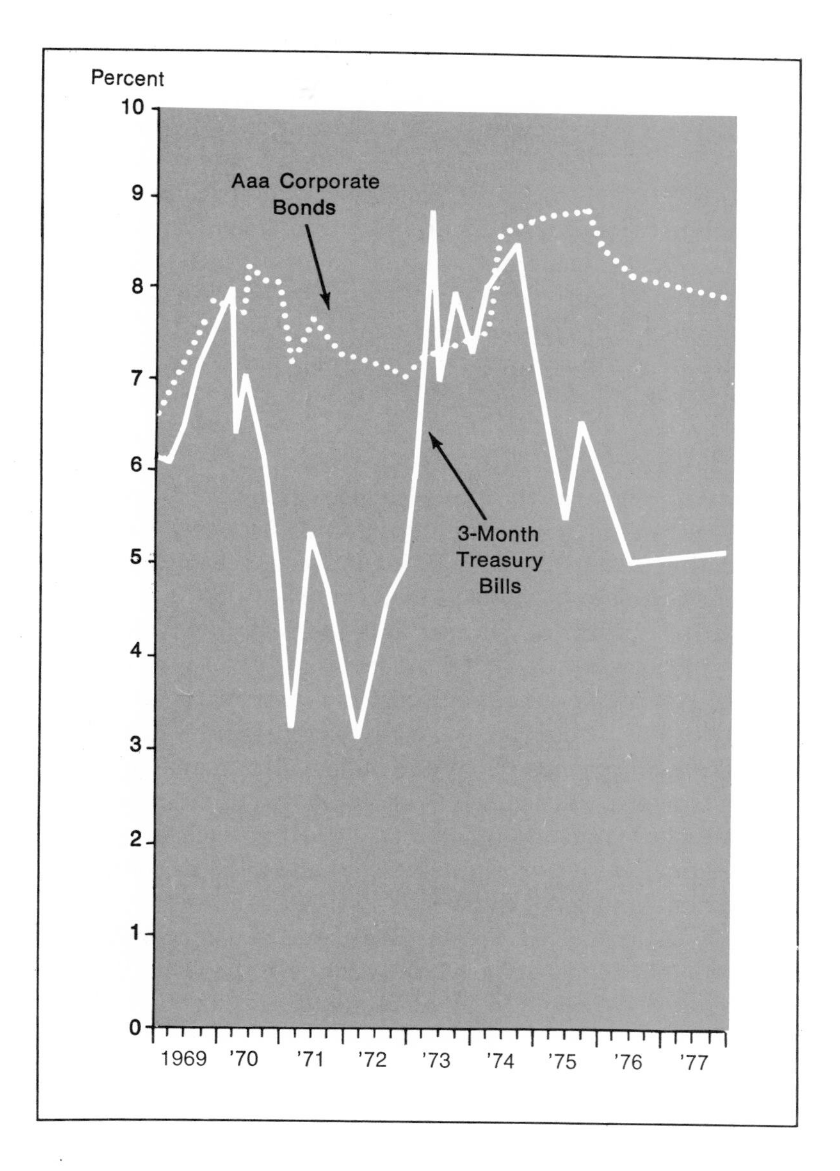

Sources: Federal Reserve Board, Moody's Investors Service, United States League of Savings Associations

sion in 1934, interest rates were set low to "stimulate the economy"; and this low interest policy prevailed until into the 1950s.

Treasury policy during 1976 was animated by mixed emotions. The hope was to keep interest rates reasonably low to encourage expansion of the economy and stimulate capital investment and building construction; yet the government also wanted domestic rates to be high enough to attract some of the many floating dollars away from European money markets. Fortunately for the business community, the first objective was given the priority.

Calculating true interest

Having surveyed the historical background of interest rates, we might now examine certain subtle techniques in lending money and calculating its rental charges that appear to relate to simple annual interest, but actually result in substantially higher true interest payments.

If you borrow $1,000 at 6 percent and pay back $1,060 at the end of the year, your cost is 6 percent at simple interest. But banks do not usually lend money that way. This is because many loans, and almost all personal loans from banks, are scheduled to be liquidated in an orderly manner by payments of a certain amount each month.

Assume, as in the first instance, that $1,000 were borrowed on January 1, to be fully repaid at the end of the year by budgeted payments. The bank would probably discount the loan—that is, take out the $60 (annual interest at 6 percent) in advance. In that case the borrower received not $1,000, but only $940. Then, he paid back $83.30 a month to liquidate the loan on schedule. But note that the "true" interest he was charged was nowhere near 6 percent, but actually at the rate of 11.8 percent on $1,000 for a full year. How did the rate get so high? Because, while the borrower was paying interest on $1,000, he had the use of only $940 and he did not have even the $940 for a full year since payments constantly reduced the loan principal. Actually the average amount of money at his disposal was only $470!

A second standard method of interest calculation, where the principal sum is repaid in monthly installments, is called "add on." This is used more by merchants than by commercial banks in the extension of credit. The same principal sum used above, $1,000, is increased at the outset by adding on $60 (the amount of annual interest at 6 percent) and the twelve monthly payments are $88.30 a month ($5 more than in the case of the discount loan). Actually, however, this "add-on" method is cheaper, coming to a true rate of 11.1 percent. This is because you start with the use of $1,060 instead of $940. You get more money for your money.

A third procedure is charging interest at a flat monthly rate on an unpaid balance. If this rate is 1 percent a month, it is 12 percent annually; if 1½ percent, then 18 percent per annum. These monthly rates are seldom used by commercial banks, but are quite standard among department and chain stores in the collection of open balances or revolving credits; and in connection with credit cards, as will be seen in a later chapter.

These are the common procedures in credit extension to individuals, conforming to state lending laws or federal banking regulations, or both. Above these, however, are the confiscatory rates charged by loan sharks to individuals who cannot qualify for loans on the basis of their credit standing. In every country there are unfortunate persons (1) whose incomes are exceedingly low or erratic; (2) whose family expenses are a heavy burden; (3) whose money management is inept; or (4) who are addicted to drugs, alcohol, or gambling. These people never have any extra money and never can qualify for "signature" loans, even with personal finance

Cash Income of Households
(by age of head of household in 1975)

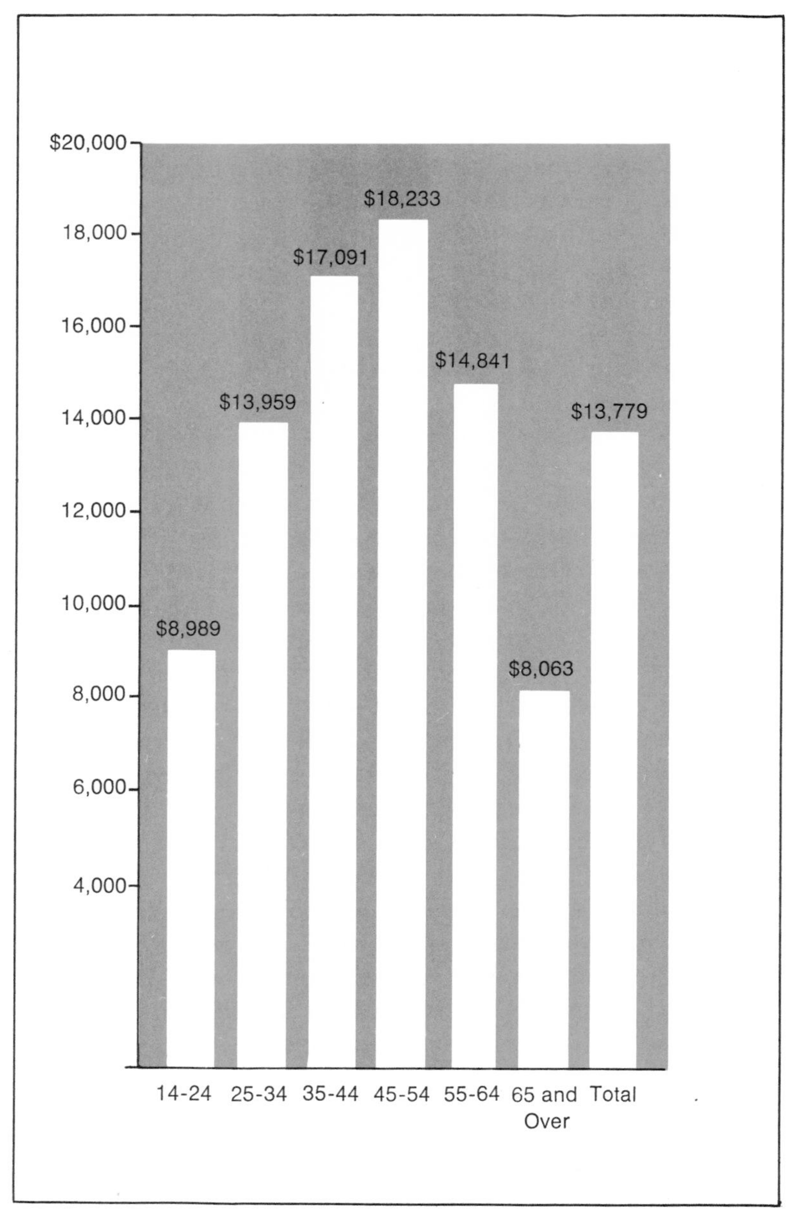

Note: Figures are for mean income, that is the total income for the group divided by the number in the group.

Sources: Bureau of the Census, National Consumer Finance Association

companies; yet they are often desperate for funds to live on. Their only available sources of cash are pawnshops and loan sharks. At either of these sources they are at the mercy of the lender, receiving meager allowance on the value of the pledged asset in the first instance and becoming the victim of human vultures in the second case. Loan shark and pawnshop interest begins at a true rate of about 40 percent, and there is no real limit among the sharks. In a loan shark contract, ultimate repayment often involves a true rate of 100 percent or more a year, with disastrous consequences in event of default, including physical violence.

The following chapters of this book will be deeply concerned with the terms, conditions, and effective interest rates on the great variety of contracts under which people borrow for needed cash; to purchase property, goods, or services; or to repay earlier loans. You may find that in buying your home on a thirty-year mortgage, you may pay considerably more in interest than the entire principal amount. You may also learn just how much of your money is spent on interest when you acquire a car, a boat, or other items by means of "easy" payments.

ACE
PUBLIC PARKING
ACE
FINANCE
Loans
PUBLIC PARKING
40
ACE

CHAPTER 3

Borrowing Money From Personal Finance Companies

About 80 percent of all adult Americans get into a financially stringent situation at some time in their lives; and millions find themselves in that situation almost continuously.

The reasons for immediate needs of cash range from due or overdue income taxes to a family accident or illness, loss of a job, hurricane damage, and even blackmail.

Whenever such an emergency arises, well-to-do people can borrow on their life insurance, sell some securities, or get a loan at the bank to tide them over. Poorer persons, however, traditionally carrying heavy family obligations, find themselves in trouble because they have meager or no assets to fall back upon. Savings, cash values in life insurance policies, and the piggy bank

Those Who Borrow From Finance Companies

(in percentages of total loans for 1975)

By Annual Income	*Number Of Loans*	*Amount Of Loans*
Less than $3,600	2.2%	1.5%
$3,600 to $5,999	10.0	6.6
$6,000 to $8,999	28.9	25.3
$9,000 to $11,999	22.0	21.5
$12,000 and over	36.9	45.1
By Age		
Less than 25 years	18.0%	15.5%
25 to 34 years	28.7	30.0
35 to 44 years	23.5	26.0
45 to 54 years	23.1	22.1
55 to 64 years	6.0	6.0
65 years and over	0.6	0.4
*By Occupation**		
Proprietors, managers, and office workers, excluding farm		6%
Craftsmen, foremen, and kindred workers		35
Operatives, laborers, and kindred workers, including farm and mine		25
Clerical and kindred workers		8
Sales persons		3
Schoolteachers		1
Professional and semiprofessional workers, excluding teachers		2
Service workers, including government civilian and military personnel		15
Occupations not reported and miscellaneous		5
By Purpose		
To consolidate existing bills		31%
Travel, vacation, education		7
Automobile purchase or repair		14
Home furnishings and appliances		4
Household repairs		5
All other purposes		39

*1974 figures latest available.

Sources: Bureau of the Census, National Consumer Finance Association

quickly run dry. After that, the next source of instant cash for most persons in the lower income brackets is the personal finance or small-loan company. These lending agencies have grown at a remarkable rate since their emergence about fifty-five years ago.

Today, the leaders in this field, Household Finance Corporation, American Investment Company, and Beneficial Loan Corporation, have among them thousands of lending branches throughout the United States, prepared to extend personal credit on the signature of an individual (sometimes accompanied by that of a spouse or cosigner). Money is swiftly available after a "credit check" establishes the worthiness of the borrower.

The principal requirements of the lender are that the borrower has: (1) a reputation for honesty and dependability, (2) a steady job, and (3) a nonmigratory history. A very high percentage of applicants receive loans.

The screening methods of personal finance companies must be quite thorough because, over a period of years, defaults on payments have averaged below 2 percent. Needless to say, these companies are extremely skilled and resourceful in collecting the money due them.

How small-loan companies developed

Whereas today there is likely to be a small-loan or personal finance office in your neighborhood with funds just waiting for you to apply, this situation is a relatively recent development in the long history of money-lending. In 1915, for example, small-loan companies did not exist; and commercial banks did not extend personal loans to people whose capacity to repay depended almost solely on a steady wage.

Banks in those days insisted on good collateral, unless the applicant was known to the bank and known to be wealthy. The ordinary family man, faced with a burdensome doctor's or hospital bill, went either to a friend

Loan Ceilings
Under State Consumer Finance Laws

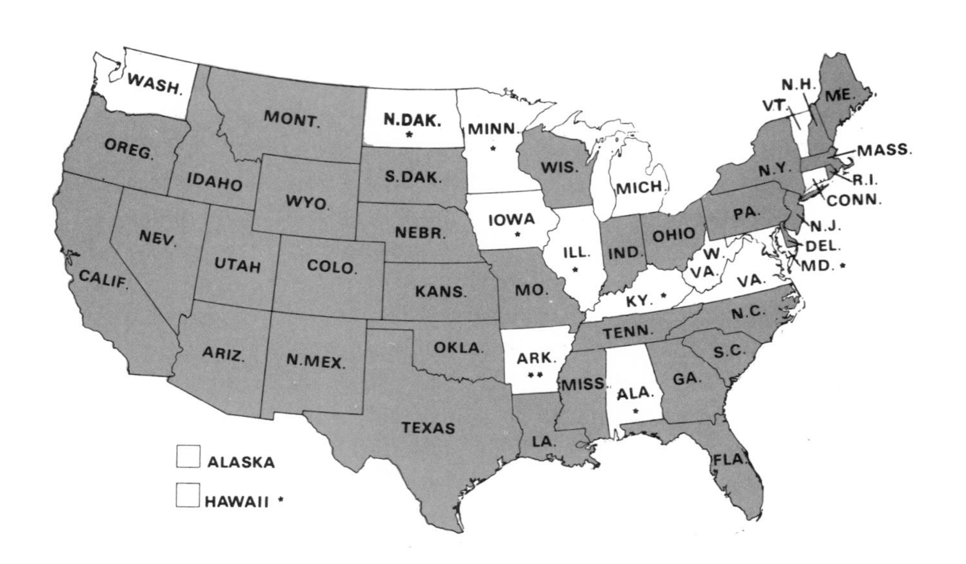

☐ Less than $2,000

■ $2,000 or over

*Permit loans of over $2,000 by finance companies under other laws.

**Arkansas does not have a consumer finance law.

Source: National Consumer Finance Association

Types of Security Accepted For Finance Company Loans
(in percentages)

	1958	*1962*	*1966*	*1969*	*1971*	*1974*	*1976*
Automobiles, household goods, and other chattels	61.1	61.2	51.4	58.7	63.2	60.7	62.1
Unsecured notes	27.4	28.9	35.2	31.1	24.0	24.6	19.6
Endorsed and/or comaker loans	2.7	2.2	2.4	2.5	2.0	2.0	4.4
Wage assignments	7.7	5.7	8.6	4.3	5.3	6.7	3.6
Real estate	0.3	0.4	0.5	0.3	1.0	1.4	3.1
Other considerations	0.8	1.6	1.9	3.1	4.5	4.6	7.2
Total	100.0	100.0	100.0	100.0	100.0	100.0	100.0

Source: National Consumer Finance Association

(usually with very little luck) or a pawnshop, or wound up in the adhesive clutches of the loan shark. He could borrow the money but at exorbitant rates—receive $80 and covenant to pay back $100 in ninety days. That is an annual interest rate of 100 percent, and yet that rate was actually low in many instances.

Because there existed such an urgent need for legitimate lending institutions to serve persons with low incomes, and because loan sharks in every big city were robbing unfortunate and often improvident people on a large scale and terrorizing them, if need be, to collect loans and interest, laws for encouraging small-loan companies were introduced in several state legislatures.

The Russell Sage Foundation, a well-endowed philanthrophic organization, was a pioneer in this effort and in 1916 was responsible for the Uniform Small-Loan Law, covering personal loans up to $300, with interest charges not to exceed 3½ percent per month. If this top rate seems high, remember that: (1) it compared with 75 to 150 percent a year regularly charged at that time by loan sharks; (2) no commercial bank extended this kind of credit to anyone; (3) such loans carried a high risk; (4) credit investigations of applicants and making collections were expensive; and (5) pursuit of delinquents was costly, particularly in relation to the small amount of money involved.

Subsequent passage of laws (modeled after this Uniform Small-Loan Law) in many states justified the vision and judgment of legislators. Hundreds of small-loan companies sprang up and flourished throughout the country.

At first they would require collateral, such as furniture or jewelry, but actual lending experience soon demonstrated that the process of earmarking this collateral, possessing it, and selling it if need be to satisfy debt defaults was inconvenient. Accordingly the general procedure was to lend, for the most part, on the signature of a borrower, or of man and wife together.

A later refinement was the guaranty of the unpaid note balance by term life insurance (usually an extra charge of 50 cents to $1 per $100 of loan) if the borrower died. In general, the interest rate was higher on smaller loans; and even today, in certain states, a true rate of 53 percent is legal and collectible on loans up to $100.

Over the years, as incomes have risen, employment has become more secure, and inflation has become a significant factor, small-loan laws in many states have been successively revised to increase the maximum size of the loan and to reduce the top rate on interest permitted, from 3½ percent to lower monthly percentages. In New York it is now possible to get a small loan of "up to $2,500."

Vital need filled

There are now over 26,000 consumer loan offices in forty-nine states and the total number of their accounts exceeds 16 million. There are no consumer loan offices in Arkansas and the District of Columbia because of laws that so severely limit interest rates as to preclude profitable operation of this type of business.

Personal lending companies have justified their existence and fill a recognized and vital economic need for a significant sector of our population. They have not put loan sharks out of business because somebody has to handle the job of supplying desperately needed cash to people whose financial status is one or more notches below steadily employed or more thrifty applicants, whom small-loan companies consistently accept.

The loan companies have an efficient and streamlined business today, benefiting from: (1) size, which enables them to borrow large amounts at prime rates from commercial banks and in the securities markets; (2) uniform accounting procedures; (3) extensive credit files with data on millions of individuals, which allow them to make swift decisions as to the acceptability of applicants; and (4) a high percentage of renewals of loans by old customers. Some customers of a seasoned small-loan company have been regular and dependable borrowers for as long as twenty years. Dealing with people like these virtually eliminates the risk element in the extension of personal loans.

Problems of small-loan companies

Small-loan companies do have their special problems, however. In a recession, defaults on loan and interest payments can increase rapidly and result in either legal or other collection costs; or the writing off of uncollectible debts nibbles away profits. In periods of high interest rates (such as 1970-4), these loan companies are inevitably caught in a squeeze between what they can charge their customers and the rates they must pay to commercial banks (down to about 11 percent in May 1976) to get the money they need for relending. The capital, surplus, and long-term debt of personal loan

Average Size of Finance Company Loans Increasing

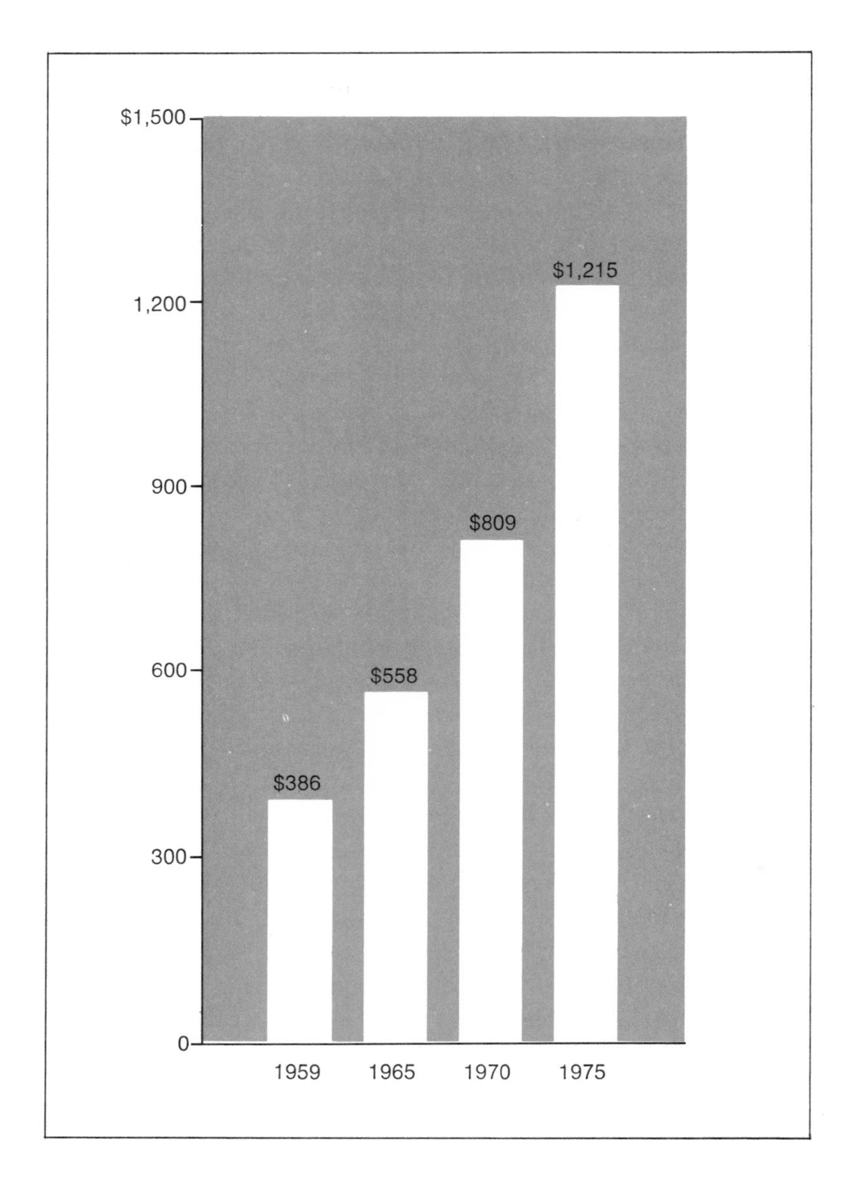

Source: National Consumer Finance Association

companies supply about two-thirds of all the money they need, so they habitually sell commercial paper and borrow substantially from commercial banks for the remainder.

This borrowing by finance companies from banks raises the question of why banks would want to lend to small-loan institutions when they might conceivably go into this business themselves. The answer is that most banks are essentially "wholesale" institutions, and would not wish to assume either the bother or the risk of lending as little as $200 to an individual whom they would regard as a "marginal" borrower at best. Further, small-loan companies have proved to be excellent risks, so that commercial banks welcome and solicit their business.

The total of personal loans in force made by finance companies in the United States was $21.3 billion at the end of 1977. So this is no small sector of the credit market.

Advantages of small loans

The advantages of dealing with a small-loan company, should you need cash in a hurry, are several. First, there is the convenience. In any metropolis there is almost certain to be a seasoned personal finance company, usually several, with branch offices around the city and one near where you live or work. These lenders advertise unremittingly; so it is easy to remember the name of a lender and the address of its branch office closest to you. (Many individuals, however, prefer to go well beyond their own area when they seek to borrow money, so that there is less chance of their neighbors somehow learning of the transaction and possibly publicizing their financial bind.)

There is little red tape or delay when you borrow from your "friendly neighborhood finance company." The application form has been compressed and simplified, and you are not asked to bare your soul. If you have steady employment, a pension, or other assurance of income; if you have lived a long time at your present address; and particularly if you own your own home, approval of your loan is almost automatic. If you are offered term life insurance on the unpaid balance, strive to get it at a charge below 50 cents per $100.

A feature of borrowing from a small-loan institution is privacy. You will usually be ushered into a small, secluded room, where you can fill out the application at leisure with no one peering over your shoulder. Customarily you will be informed within a couple of hours if you have been accepted or rejected. If all goes well, you will receive the money in cash within twenty-four hours.

It is this simplicity, privacy, and speed that have made personal finance companies so acceptable to so many people. You know how much you can borrow, what it will cost you, and how many months you have in which to pay it back. Loans usually run up to thirty-six months. The interest you pay will depend on the laws of the state in which you borrow and the amount of your loan. Count on paying an effective annual rate of 36 percent on small loans and as low as 15 percent for larger loans.

Many satisfied customers

Thousands of people who have been satisfied with the treatment received at a personal loan office continue to borrow there even when they qualify, in due course, for the much larger credit and lower interest rates available at commercial banks.

In recent years, several major commercial bank holding companies in metropolitan areas have themselves acquired personal finance companies in order to (1) share in the rewarding profits historically gleaned in this field, (2) reach a group of borrowers who comprise a sort of "prep school" for larger credit lines later on, and (3) avail themselves of a profitable outlet for their own expanding lending capability.

Personal loan companies have been zealous and liberal with their advertising and promotion programs, and have had excellent results from these efforts. They encourage you by radio and television to borrow to do your Christmas shopping, to finance a vacation trip, to purchase clothing, to pay your dentist, or to consolidate a number of debts into a single loan to be repaid by one monthly payment.

Also, after the loan has been whittled down by several payments, they will write you a note telling you what a dependable and responsible individual you are, and suggesting subtly that you increase the loan to the amount it was originally and thereby enjoy the immediate use of extra cash. This approach often proves successful. Another variation is to tell you that you have so faithfully and punctually met your payment obligations that you now qualify for their "big economy package"—a much larger loan than your original one, at lower rates and with a longer repayment period. They will not fail to inform you, almost instantly, whenever a new state law permits them to increase the loan limits to their clients —particularly to you.

The major drawbacks of small loans, namely the limitation on size and the high interest rates, apparently have not been an impediment to their growth. The titans in the field, Household Finance, Beneficial Loan, and American Investment, have grown rapidly and consistently, and have increased their net profits steadily for decades. As their permitted loan limits have risen, they have been able to offer competition to consumer installment companies by financing the purchase of cars, household appliances, home improvements, and small pleasure boats. And they have definitely narrowed the

The Increase in Consumer Installment Debt To Finance Companies

1965

Total: $23.9 billion

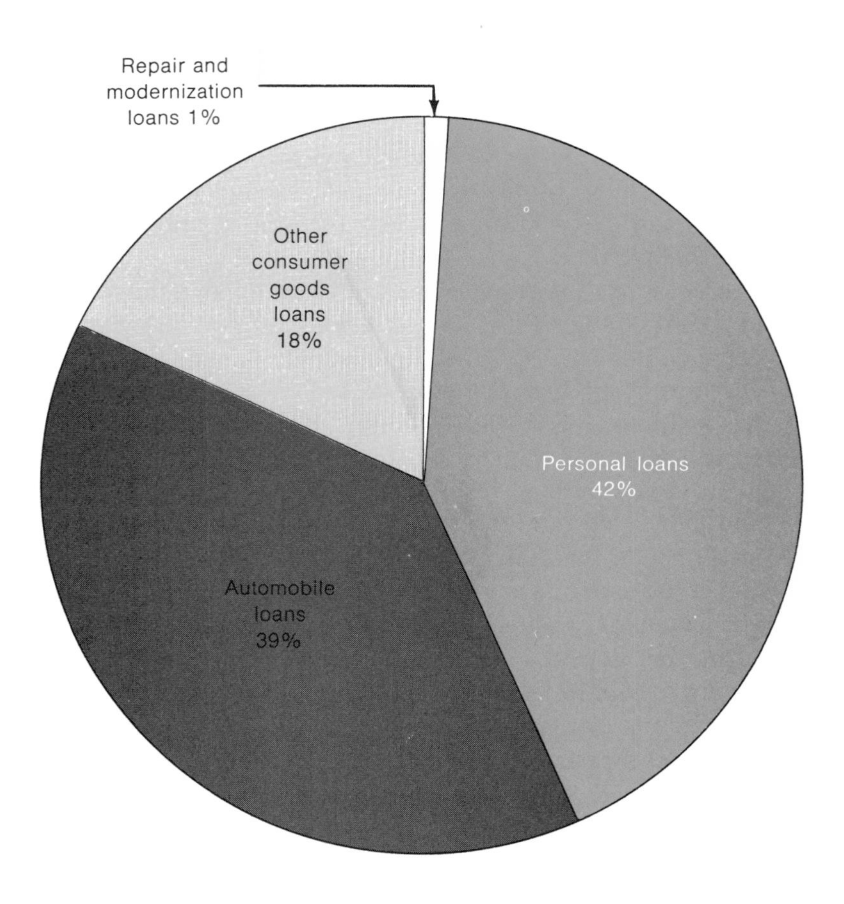

Sources: Federal Reserve Board, National Consumer Finance Association

The Increase in Consumer Installment Debt To Finance Companies

1975

Total: $38.9 billion

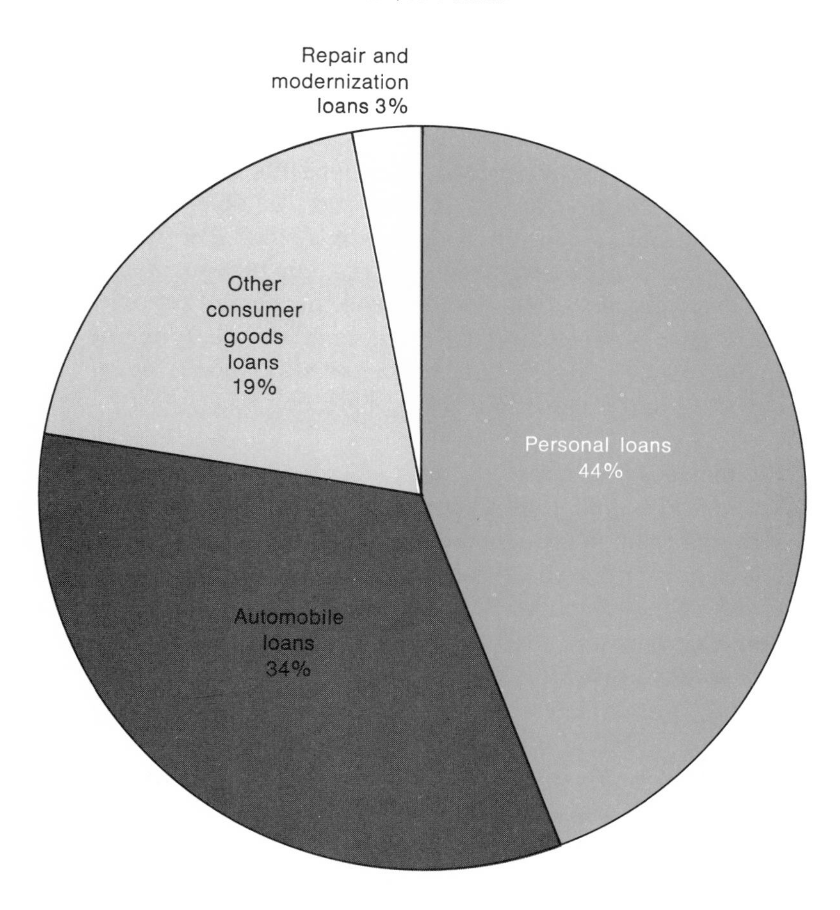

business prospects of loan sharks, who in the nineteenth century had this personal loan business all to themselves in many states, and conducted it as a racket and a monopoly.

One borrower's story

One man, after borrowing regularly from a personal finance company, so greatly improved his income level that he built up a surplus of cash and was able to buy a considerable amount of the company's stock. By this investment he increased his net worth 1,000 percent within the next ten years due to an increase in the market price of the shares, stock dividends, and cash income. Ignoring Shakespeare's advice, "neither a borrower nor a lender be," this man prospered by being both.

Regulations outlined

The rates and limits shown in Appendix II are abstracted from existing enactments in the various states. Laws governing these sectors of personal credit have been frequently amended, and in the inflationary economic climate since 1970, upper lending limits have been increased in several instances.

The highest current limit, $50,000, is available in Oregon. Idaho, Maine, and Utah have a $40,000 limit; Indiana goes up to $32,500; and $25,000 is the limit in Colorado, Kansas, Louisiana, Oklahoma, and Wyoming. It is from these states that "executive loans" (generally calling for 18 percent annual interest) are offered by mail, often by personal loan subsidiaries of large out-of-state bank holding companies.

In almost every state the top legal interest rate applies to the smallest loan accepted; rates are usually lowered as the size of the loan increases.

The states vary in the types of interest calculations they approve. Some permit "add-on"; some "discount";

and some authorize use of revolving credit, with interest at defined monthly rates applying to unpaid balances.

One attempt to make regulation of all lending institutions closely similar is the Uniform Consumer Credit Code drafted by the Commission on Uniform State Laws. Nine states have adopted versions of this code.

Certain consumer-oriented congressmen believe that a rate as high as 3 percent a month borders on the usurious, regardless of the size of the loan or the risk involved; and there have been some proposals that federal legislation be introduced to set uniform nationwide rates and limits, rather than continuing the present patchwork pattern of assorted state regulations.

Interest rates in the United States reached historic heights in 1974. In particular the "prime rate," when it went above 11 percent, became notably burdensome to consumer loan companies. They are constant borrowers at commercial banks; and if they have to pay, say, 12 percent for their money, and lend it to individuals at 15 percent, the return on their money is inadequate to meet operational costs and to generate profits at acceptable levels. This squeeze also reduces the profit of small-loan companies because any higher interest rates they may pass on to their borrowers tend to reduce their total business volume.

Persistence of high bank loan rates over a long period of time would almost certainly result in legislative amendments raising the allowable interest rates on personal loans in many states.

NATIONAL
BANK
SIDEWALK TELLER
203
NATIONAL
BANK

CHAPTER 4

Borrowing Money From Banks

Until 1928 personal loans were rarely made by commercial banks. The business accent of these institutions was on loans to partnerships and corporations, and to wealthy individuals whose personal resources or available collateral made them sound risks. Even these well-to-do borrowers were usually asked to pledge some blue chip stocks or prime bonds if they sought a personal loan.

Small checking accounts were not largely solicited by commercial banks; and the idea of making money by charging so much per check on mini-balance accounts was undreamed of. Also, the concept that a man might be a safe risk for a modest "signature" loan, with only his salary as the security for its repayment, apparently did not find favor with bank officers of that era. Indeed, credit was something available to rather exclusive groups. In those days if you were eligible to borrow at a bank, usually you did not need to.

In the late 1920s, however, banks, which heretofore had carried on their business in impressive downtown buildings of granite or marble, began to establish branches in different parts of the cities; and new banks were chartered in great numbers to serve rapidly growing communities and suburbs. Further, nationwide prosperity and the increase in per-capita incomes brought millions of families up to a level where they could maintain acceptable balances in checking accounts and enjoy the convenience of paying their bills by checks instead of with cash or money orders, as before. Less traditionally minded bank officers emerged who saw this growing middle class as a profitable and rapidly expanding market for a more comprehensive line of banking services, including personal loans and personal trusts.

After watching for a few years the growth and profitability of small-loan companies (and incidentally lending money to them), perceptive bank officials recognized that a modest loan, made only on the basis of the character of the borrower and his steady employment, was a sound loan and could prove profitable if interest charges were somewhat higher than those paid by business borrowers. They felt that 2 or 3 percent over the bank's "prime rate" to its most solvent borrowers was worth considering for loans to individuals, even though investigation of the less well-off loan applicant might be more costly.

The first major bank in the United States to open a personal loan department was the National City Bank of New York (now renamed Citibank, the dominant subsidiary of Citicorp). That step was taken in 1928. Citibank remains a leader in personal loan business, but thousands of other commercial banks across the land entered this field. They learned that properly screened personal loans yield higher net returns to the bank for each dollar of credit extended than do traditional commercial loans, and that individual defaults average, over a period of years, less than 1 percent. Further, a good percentage of borrowers become regular depositors in thrift or checking accounts, buy travelers' checks, join Christmas clubs, or name the bank as trustee in their wills.

The personal loan departments, originally set up in the home offices of the banks, have spread to a myriad of branch offices. Personal loans are now among the best earning assets in a bank's portfolio. At the end of 1975, when installment personal loans in the United States totaled $44.7 billion, commercial banks accounted for 31.3 percent of the volume.

Individual loan procedures

People who borrow from banks usually have higher incomes and more valuable personal assets than those who patronize small-loan companies. The bank loan may be arranged by a present depositor or in conjunction with opening a new account. The new customer may have been attracted to a bank by its advertising of personal loan arrangements, may have had a friend or relative who was well pleased with the service, or may just have dropped in at a bank most convenient for him. In any event he will generally find himself welcome, and courteously served by an intelligent and informed credit officer.

The applicant usually will be asked routine questions about age and marital status; place and length of employment, position held, and approximate income; home ownership, if any, and size of mortgage or monthly rental payments; other indebtedness; and possibly possession of realty other than a home; and marketable securities. Also requested will be the amount of loan desired, duration preferred, and whether notices should be sent to home or office.

Modern banking practice is to stress personal income and character in considering the application and in approving or rejecting it. An applicant's payment history on prior loans, charge accounts, and auto or appliance purchases (if such have been acquired on installments) may be investigated.

If you have delayed in paying department store accounts, had court judgments against you, ever been bankrupt, or been criminally or scandalously involved, your application may be denied. If your record is clean, and the amount of the loan and monthly payments are sensibly proportioned to your income, your loan should be approved.

You will seldom be granted a signature loan totaling more than 20 percent of your gross annual income; and you will be flirting with trouble if the total of your interest and debt monthly repayments—mortgage, car, and personal loan—exceed 20 percent of your gross income.

Borrowing a desired sum may be relatively easy, but repaying it can cause anguish if you have high family expenditures, children attending school or college, and social expenses such as golf or pool club memberships.

If you assume too heavy a burden of personal debt, the pressure and anxiety may affect your health, your performance on the job, and your personal equilibrium. If your debts trigger a drinking or gambling problem, or make it necessary for you to moonlight for extra income, you may suffer a nervous breakdown. So when you take out a personal loan, have a good reason for doing so, borrow no more than you need, and pay it back on schedule.

Bank loan details

At bank personal loan departments the upper limit usually is $5,000. The loan may run, depending on your preference, from twelve to thirty-six months. It will be a loan reflecting the rate of interest prevailing at the time you sign for it.

Suppose you request $3,000 and plan to repay it over a twenty-four-month period. At a 6 percent true rate, interest for two years will be $360; so the total loan will be $3,360. When discounted, that will supply you with exactly $3,007.20 in instant cash; and over the life of the loan, assuming your prompt monthly payments, the effective rate will be 10.89 percent. This contract will also include declining-balance term life insurance.

Depending on the policy of the bank and the level of your salary, you might get a top-limit loan as high as $10,000, but this would be far above the average for single signature personal loans at commercial banks.

The seemingly high charges for interest, running up to 18 percent, are not fraudulent or usurious. They are entirely legal, and reflect standard banking practice predicated on three factors: (1) individual credit is costlier to investigate than are business loans; (2) collection procedures, in event of default, can be slow, and legal costs, if necessary, are expensive; and (3) a "good loan" from the bank's standpoint is one that is methodically reduced at regular intervals.

Moreover, you, as an individual in quest of credit, have to pay the "going rate" or you will not get the loan. When you borrow you are in competition with millions of other individuals with a "liquidity problem," corporations planning to expand their plants or enlarge their inventories, and municipalities and states needing to build public buildings, sewers, or highways. The loan for $3,000 outlined earlier can appear reasonable or costly, depending on the prevailing interest rates at the time.

If you are not over age sixty-five, the declining balance of the loan is covered by term life insurance (which you pay for) ; and some policies are available to pay off the loan should you have an accident or become disabled so that you are unable to work.

The $3,000 loan described is quite typical, and the great proportion of all personal loans made by banks in the United States are similarly structured, and offered with varying amounts, maturities, and interest rates.

Home-improvement loans

A popular variation is the home-improvement loan. This may finance a new kitchen, an extra bathroom, painting, siding, or some similar project. It is calculated quite like any other personal loan, except that it is usually larger in amount and extends over a longer period of time. Most home-improvement loans run for five years. They are not granted after you have made the improvement. You must give the bank assurance and evidence that the sum advanced is being, or will be, used exclusively for the specific and agreed-on home improvement and not to buy a racehorse or take a Caribbean cruise or for some other unapproved purpose. Usually the bank will ask to see plans for the proposed improvement.

In New York State home-improvement loans run as high as $15,000 with a maximum length of ten years and up to 12 percent interest (there is a slightly lower rate for loans of five years or less). The amount of the loan, maturity, and rate will vary according to different state laws.

The total of installment home-improvement loan holdings of financial institutions was over $10 billion at the end of 1977, showing that this is indeed an important sector of the consumer credit market. Loans are either conventional or guaranteed by the Federal Housing Administration (FHA). Banks offer both varieties and the average amount of home-improvement loans in 1977 was over $5,000.

Overdraft loans

In recent years banks have developed another level of personal loans that has proved both desirable to depositors and profitable to the bank. It is the overdraft loan. Until fairly recently, if a checking account was overdrawn, an inadequately covered check bounced—that is, it was returned to the issuer, marked "insufficient funds." This proved not only embarrassing to the issuer but irritating to the payee; and it also involved an additional debit for the account of three or four dollars to cover the bank's handling charges.

Under the present arrangement, the bank will accept and honor a check drawn for more money than the account contains, providing the amount does not exceed an agreed-in-advance limit; and the overdraft will become a loan, payable over the next ninety days, with usually 1 percent per month as a flat interest charge. This way the depositor need not fear a telephone call from the bank, telling him to come right over and "deposit enough money to cover." Rather, the check is honored in the normal manner, and he can take his time in making up the deficit. Generally this overdraft loan is limited to between $300 and $500; but in the case of depositors who regularly keep larger balances or who subscribe to special credit cards for executives, the automatic open-credit line may range up to $2,500 or more.

Arrangements for overdrafts may be made with respect to either special or regular checking accounts, depending on the policy of the bank. Other related loan plans reserve credit of a given maximum amount and provide the customer with a book of checks. He need not maintain a checking account balance at all, but simply

Credit Card Debts And Check Credit Plans At Commercial Banks

(in millions of dollars)

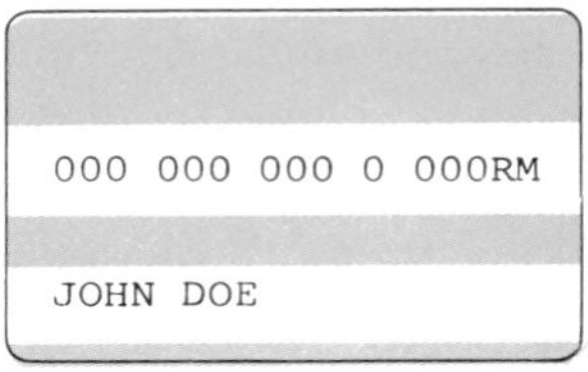

000 000 000 0 000RM

JOHN DOE

	1974	1975	1976
Credit Cards Outstanding	$8,281	$9,501	$11,351

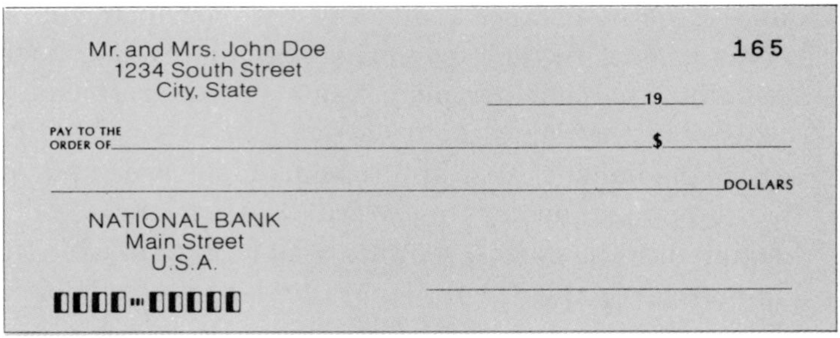

Mr. and Mrs. John Doe
1234 South Street
City, State

165

19

PAY TO THE ORDER OF $

DOLLARS

NATIONAL BANK
Main Street
U.S.A.

	1974	1975	1976
Check Credit Outstanding	$2,797	$2,810	$3,041

Source: Federal Reserve Board

draw on the credit by writing a check, at which time interest at the rate of 1½ percent a month will apply on the loan thus created (to all intents and purposes, a simple overdraft).

For customers in the higher income brackets, some banks will establish an open credit line for as much as $5,000. This may never be used, but it is there and waiting and acts as an automatic defense should one need to write a sizable check when account funds are low. The advantage of a credit line is that it does not require the submission of a loan application or a financial statement each time a credit extension is sought.

Loans by mail

In 1973 there appeared on the scene a new variation in lending: a rapid, quite confidential service tailored to the needs of executives and professional people.

The lending agencies providing this swift credit (completely arranged by mail and without need for any personal appearance) are, in many cases, subsidiaries of bank holding companies. They offer large loans (up to $20,000) on personal signatures and without collateral; but you must have a high income and your credit rating must be solid to withstand the searching investigation which will surely be made before you get your money.

The actual offices from whence this credit comes need not be in large metropolitan centers, but will surely be located in states that have legalized this sort of loan.

You will see newspaper advertisements of these companies listing addresses in many inland cities. You can borrow for twenty-four months or up to five years. Suppose you are interested in obtaining a loan of either $5,000 or $10,000, and plan to pay the money back in monthly installments for sixty months. Here is how it would work out:

Cash Advance	*Monthly Repayment*	*Total Finance Charge*	*Your Total Payment*
$ 5,000	$126.96	$2,617.60	$ 7,617.60
$10,000	$253.93	$5,235.80	$15,235.80

(This includes term life if you are not over fifty-five.)

The amount you pay for the use of this money is so large because this table is calculated on the basis of a true interest rate of 18 percent. Hundreds of such loans are made every day to people whose credit is satisfactory but who, for some reason, prefer not to obtain the loan in their own locality. This elite credit accommodation is highly profitable for the subsidiary of a big bank holding company; and it indirectly permits the institution to develop a banking business in many sections of the country beyond the boundaries of the state in which its commercial banking operations are carried out. Loans of this sort, however, can be made in very few states. (For example, Tennessee has a law limiting maximum interest to a 10 percent rate.)

The foregoing outlines bank credit arrangements which simplify application procedures, accelerate the delivery of cash to individuals, and offer many options in repayment scheduling. These arrangements are designed to solve problems in personal financial liquidity. There is a price for all of these fountains of funds: interest charges, which may badly dent your budget.

These loans are designed to deliver cash to borrowers without reference to any particular purchase, except in the case of home improvements. We will later discuss a different type of bank credit, and bank credit cards, which permit deferred or installment payments on the purchase of goods or services. Installment purchase contracts with "finance charges" (actually, interest) built in are regarded not as loans but as conditional sales agreements, depending for their ultimate settlement not only on the income of the buyer, but also on a legal right to repossess the item purchased in the event of default on payments due. Installment sales flourish in a credit world of their own.

PAWNSH
1901
LOANS
on· Cameras
Watches·Jewelry

CHAPTER 5

Other Sources of Loans

While banks and finance companies are the principal vendors of loans for cash or for the purchase of merchandise, there are several other sources to which people hastily turn to meet urgent financial needs. Of these perhaps the most commonly used, and the one most likely to open the door to personal harassment and hostility, is the money of a friend or a relative.

Borrowing from friends often takes place in poker games when one of the group, finding that he owes more than he can pay at the end of the evening, writes an I.O.U. to the winner. If it is a small amount, say $25 or $50, it will probably be paid, usually after a little prodding from the unsecured creditor. But if the game was for high stakes and the scribbled evidence of indebtedness runs to $100 or more, there is almost invariably trouble. The loser may later contend it was "just a friendly game," and try to avoid paying the debt by this ploy; or he may make a cash offer of less than the amount of the I.O.U., hoping to settle the debt in this way. If the debt is sizable, say $500, chances are that the debtor is chronically in financial trouble, possibly behind on his taxes and car installments as well as his gambling debts.

In any event, the chances of the large I.O.U. being paid off in full are slim; there is likely to be hostility between the noteholder and the losing player; and most probably the debtor will be drummed out of the poker group.

Prudent card players do not play in games where the stakes are too high for them; and when their cash runs out, they quit and go home. A loan to defray card debts is one of the most unwise in the entire spectrum of credit extensions.

Another common situation where a friend or more frequently a relative is approached for a loan results from a personal or family emergency—illness, accident, putting up bail, or losing a job. Probably a good friend is more likely than a relative to produce the needed cash; but often recourse to both is necessary. The climate of this kind of borrowing is tense. It is demeaning for the borrower to plead for a loan, and the percentage of success is low. Often the person approached refuses to lend the money, and accompanies his refusal with an unwelcome lecture on prudence, thrift, and the need to prepare for emergencies. Or he may plead that he is short of funds himself, although this may not be the case.

Even if a loan is obtained from a friend or relative, paying back usually causes trouble. There may be the question of interest on the loan; sometimes even a pledge of something valuable is involved; and there is often increasingly nasty dunning by the creditor. Repayments of loans made within families have a miserable record.

This kind of borrowing has a long and sordid history of marring or destroying amity or even civility between the debtor and friend or relative. Borrowing this way can hardly be recommended.

Life insurance loans

More than 130 million Americans own permanent life insurance policies, and the values built up in these represent a major financial bulwark for the average American family.

All the standard straight, or whole-life, policies and endowment contracts generate what are called policy reserves, built up by systematic premium payments. These policy reserves generally begin during the second year the policy is in force, although a few companies establish them in the first year. Reserves are actually cash values available to the policyholder either by loan or outright withdrawal. The total amount of available cash in the policy increases each year and with each premium payment.

The advantages of borrowing on the cash values in life insurance policies are: there is no credit investigation; you need not state the purpose of the loan; you can get the money on very short notice (usually within two or three days); there is no set time for you to pay it back (and you need never do so); and the interest charged on the loan is spelled out in the policy, and is often below current bank loan rates.

In policies issued several years ago the stipulated rate was 5 percent. Newer policies have defined a 6 percent rate, and, prompted by the inflation during 1970-4, many states have been authorizing loan rates as high as 8 percent to be written into policies. Ahead, no doubt, will be some new standardization, possibly stating in each policy a loan rate, related to the prevailing prime rate, at the time of borrowing.

Increase in loans on policies

A considerable concern about interest rates on policy loans has surfaced recently because many policyholders have been borrowing on their policies at 6 or 8 percent rather than from banks where cash loans cost 10 to 12 percent.

Life insurance companies have not welcomed these virtual raids on their current assets because they prefer to retain these funds for their own investment in the current bond market at more than 8 percent and in this way expand their earnings and their surpluses. Also, the sums borrowed may never be paid back; and those who borrow heavily on their policies tend to cancel them later on. The insurance actually in force in any policy is reduced by the amount of the loan and by any interest charged against the policy. If the principal amount is substantially reduced, many insured persons prefer to let their policy lapse and buy a new one with the full face amount in force.

The borrowing on policies has been of real concern to the life insurance industry, significantly reducing its invested assets, and frequently resulting in use of the funds to buy cars or appliances or other consumer goods rather than to preserve family thrift programs. At the end of January 1977 policy loans in the United States totaled $27.5 billion and represented 9.85 percent of life insurers' assets. Between 1945 and 1965 this figure never went above 5 percent. The record high was 18.3 percent—set in 1932 during the Great Depression.

The actual procedures of policy borrowing are simple. You file a loan agreement at a company office, requesting immediate payment of all, or a named amount of, current cash values in your policy. This application is rushed to the home office of the company and rapidly processed, so that you receive your check in a few days.

Remember, however, that the loan reduces the face

How Life Insurance Policy Loans Have Soared

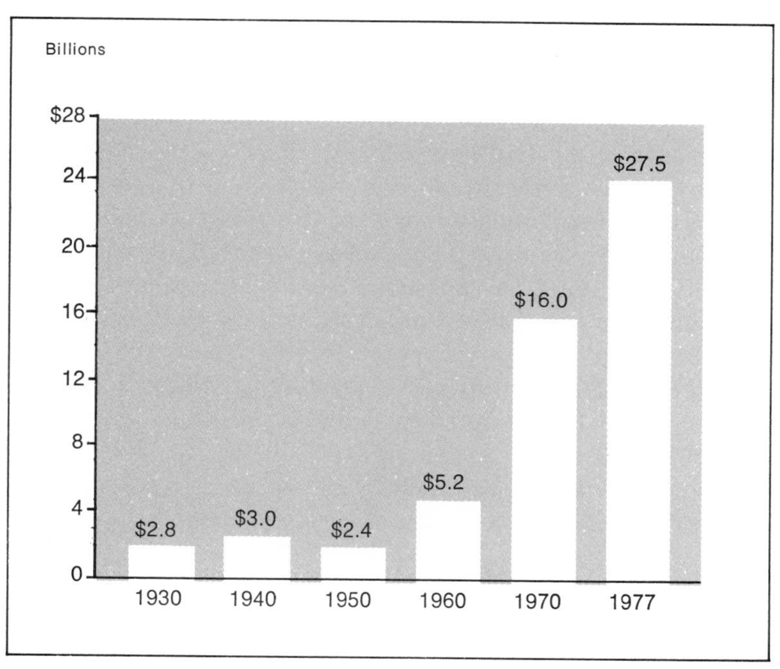

Sources: *Spectator Year Book,* Institute of Life Insurance

amount on the policy, and also involves annual interest at the stated rate. The temptation is to make no attempt to repay the loan, since there is no obligation to do so; and even to pay the interest on the loan by charging it, too, against the cash values. If you continue to pay premiums, the policy's cash value will, of course, build up again by the reserves allocated and by the application of policy dividends if the contract is in a mutual company.

When you acquired your life insurance policy you had in mind the need of a certain amount of protection. You may still need this; so if you have borrowed, say, $3,000 on a $10,000 policy, plan to pay the money back as soon as you can to restore full insurance coverage.

Thrift accounts

Another almost instant way of raising cash also involves "borrowing from yourself." If you have a thrift account in a bank or savings and loan association, you can borrow swiftly against your balance on deposit. Many people prefer to do this rather than to draw out the actual cash, because they know that if they withdraw the money they are unlikely to pay it back. They can obtain what is called a "passbook" loan—borrow a certain amount and pay interest on it at a rate 10 to 20 percent higher than the regular rate of interest currently being paid on thrift accounts in the particular institution. Here again, the money is quickly available; no credit investigation is required; and there are no inquiries about the purpose for which the money will be used. And again, there is no pressure on you to repay the loan.

Credit unions

Probably less is known about credit unions than about most other major lending organizations. Credit unions are cooperative nonprofit financial institutions formed usually by people with some common bond—membership in a union, fraternal organization, or church; employment in the same firm or in the teaching profession; or service in a branch of the armed forces.

The first credit union was opened in New Hampshire in 1909. The idea caught on rapidly and growth has been dramatic in recent years. By the end of 1977 there were 22,448 credit unions (12,752 federal and 9,696 state) in the United States. Combined assets totaled $54 billion. With a membership total of 36,512,000, credit unions range in size from 200 members to the Navy Federal Credit Union, which has over 430,000 members and possesses more than $650 million in assets.

To be eligible for membership in a credit union, you are expected to share in the common bond that identifies its membership. Then you make an opening payment ($5 minimum), for which you get a share, and pay dues of possibly 25 cents. The additional payments you may make purchase additional shares; and your savings build up much like those in a bank or savings and loan association.

The funds in the treasury of a credit union are designed for one purpose: lending money at modest interest to members who need it. In 1976 credit union loans were divided as follows: loans for durable goods, 47.5 percent; personal loans, 31.5 percent; repair and modernization loans, 11.4 percent; real estate loans, 6 percent; and business loans, 3.6 percent.

The average loan is about $1,741, but credit unions can lend up to $2,500 on single signatures (some unions have no fixed maximum) and more in the cases of comaker or home mortgage loans. Interest on loans is limited to a 12 percent annual rate. Some credit unions may lend at lower rates, especially on secured loans.

Because they are nonprofit institutions and usually are operated at low cost in unpretentious headquarters, credit unions are able to offer loans to members at lower rates than the profit-making lenders.

Credit unions may be formed under either state or federal charters. All federal credit unions, and many state-chartered ones, have share insurance (similar to deposit insurance in a bank) of up to $40,000 on each account, through the National Credit Union Administration. Usually a minimum of 200 members is sought for the opening of a new credit union.

Credit unions reward their members with dividends on fully paid up shares; the maximum allowable interest rate is 7 percent. Dividends are derived primarily from the earnings on loans made to members. In 1976 dividends averaged 6.15 percent. Some credit unions also distribute profits in the form of interest rebates.

Those who belong to a credit union benefit by having at hand a thrift institution at which they may save regularly, often by payroll deduction plans; and borrow readily on nothing more than their own signatures, at rates generally below those of commercial banks or personal loan companies. Loans by credit unions are approved swiftly, with little red tape; and can be made, in cases of emergency, after regular business hours. Simplicity of procedure is assured because members borrow in effect from their peers; from people they know and who know them, because they work together or belong to the same organization. Loans range from short term to five years for unsecured loans and up to ten years for secured loans.

Credit unions not only offer a most accessible source of cash loans, but may extend credit to borrowers who might be turned down by other lending institutions. Credit union members have proved to be excellent risks, and their percentage of loan losses is probably lower than for competing institutions.

When seeking a low-cost loan, a credit union is a good place to go. If you cannot qualify for membership in an existing one, you and your associates may be able to form a new credit union. Further, many of the established credit unions now seek to broaden their membership to include people of good character and financial integrity in their communities.

Pawnshops

Pawnshops are among the oldest sources of instant cash, although less used than formerly because there are now so many other professional lenders and fewer people in desperate straits. As they have been for centuries, pawnshops remain a place of last resort for those in deep financial trouble. People do not deal with a pawnshop if they have life insurance, a savings account, or a car on which they can borrow money. They pawn their possessions when there is no other way to raise cash, and the collateral they are able to offer would not generally be accepted by any other kind of professional lender.

Pawnshops have not changed much in their appearance over the years. In the downtown area of many cities you can still see the dimly-lit shops with three gold balls hanging over their doors and a bizarre assortment of items in their windows: a bronze bust, a battered guitar, a hi-fi set, a microscope, an expensive fishing rod and reel, a pair of binoculars, a typewriter, a wristwatch, and a shabby fur coat. All these articles are in the window because people have pledged them for loans and have not been able to muster the cash to redeem them.

This is how a pawn loan works: A person down on his luck enters a pawnshop toting, say, a Japanese camera that cost over $200 when new. The appraiser examines it and accords it a loan value of $50. The applicant is shocked at being offered so little for it, but he has no alternative, so he takes the $50 and gets a pawn ticket. He must pay back the $50 within a year, plus interest at a rate of probably 20 percent or more (it can run much higher). If he cannot raise the money within the time period specified, the pawnbroker is permitted to sell the camera. The broker will usually come out ahead in this transaction, as he will lend only 50 to 75 percent of what the camera would probably bring at auction. A bargain hunter visiting the pawnshop to buy unredeemed wares is quite certain to pay a price for the camera that will give the pawnbroker a profit.

Not all pawnshops are located in somewhat seedy neighborhoods. The world's biggest pawnshop is believed to be Paul Kaskel and Sons on swank Fifty-Seventh Street in New York City. Here, a well-dressed stockbroker, whose net worth has been critically eroded by a bear market, may furtively enter to borrow a few thousand dollars on a pearl necklace or a chinchilla coat. It is quite likely that the proprietor knows the man because he has visited the shop before on a similar mission.

A more typical case would be a man coming into the shop with a wristwatch costing originally $300 or more. The man would be asked to identify himself by a passport, driver's license, or some other government-issued document, and to give his address. Then the wristwatch offered as collateral would be appraised and given a loan value of, say, $100. The borrower would then surrender the watch, receive the $100, and sign an obligation to repay the $100 (and redeem the collateral) on or before the end of six months, and to pay interest accruing at the rate of 3 percent a month in the interim. The borrower would be notified at the end of six months and given ten additional days in which to pay up, or to exercise the privilege of extending the loan for another six months, with interest reduced to 2 percent a month. If he chooses the latter option, at the end of twelve months the borrower would again be notified. If he did not repay the loan within ten days, the pawnbroker would have the right to sell the watch at a public auction and keep the proceeds to satisfy the loan and interest accrued.

That is the way the transaction would be handled in New York City. Elsewhere, pawnshops may operate differently under the laws of the various states. Interest charges may be considerably higher, and after the due date for repayment, items may be sold directly to individuals and not necessarily by public auction.

Pawnshops are a credit haven of last resort for several reasons: so little money can be raised there on the average collateral offered; the pledged assets are often really needed by the owners; interest rates are high; and the borrower may never get his collateral back, which can be painful, particularly if the item has sentimental value.

Pawnshops have been featured in novels and dramas, and are replete with human interest, but for most people today there are usually more attractive places in which to borrow money. In times of economic depression pawnshops flourish. They have not been in an expansion phase during the generally prosperous period since 1946.

Loan sharks

One of the oldest entrepreneurs recorded in history is the moneylender. Dating from Biblical times are reports of financially tormented people, hopelessly in debt, who turned in desperation to gouging moneylenders. These lenders made it a point to keep liquid resources on hand and systematically made loans at rates as high as the traffic would bear.

Whether in India or China, on the New York waterfront, or in the poorer districts of Detroit, Saint Louis, or Birmingham, troubled individuals have turned to unscrupulous loan sharks for help, only to be hounded into nervous breakdowns, or maimed or killed by enforcers if the debtors got behind in their payments. Once in debt to a loan shark, the borrower may not be able to extricate himself for years, often having difficulty in even keeping up with the interest charges, much less being able to decrease the amount of the loan itself.

The pages of literature are full of characters who, due to accident, illness, family problems, or addiction to liquor or gambling have fallen into the clutches of loan sharks. Unable to repay, they find their debts extended, enlarged, and compounded by high interest, and they remain in debt for years or even for life. The fictional borrower is afraid to turn to law enforcement officers, lest he be beaten up by mobsters. Meanwhile, his debt may increase, by usurious interest charges and delayed payment penalties, to an amount twice or three times the original amount borrowed.

Such cases still occur in the United States. People on the lower rungs of the income ladder, migratory, seasonal, or intermittent workers, compulsive gamblers, those on the welfare rolls, or chronic spendthrifts may become so desperate for money that they turn to loan sharks, usually because their credit status is so low that they cannot obtain money through legitimate lending channels, and they know of no other agencies to help them.

Loan sharks have extensive operations, especially in states where there are no effective small-loan laws or usury restrictions; and even in states that have such regulations they do a flourishing business outside the law. They charge interest at high rates and interest on unpaid interest. Sometimes they insist that their clients buy credit life insurance at exorbitant premium rates to assure payment if the borrower dies. All this increases the burden of the borrower.

Here is how a loan shark operates. He usually has a very efficient sales department. He may have friends or representatives in a factory, waterfront, slum, or racetrack area. He may arrange to have cards or leaflets handed to workers as they leave piers, factories, warehouses, or slaughter yards; or at barrooms, fraternal organizations, or political clubhouses. Most of the loans will be small—$25, $50, $100, or $200. Short maturities are preferred by the loan shark because loans are then harder to repay and more likely to result in extensions and the piling up of interest. His real aim is to keep a borrower in permanent debt so that a client becomes almost an annuity, never freeing himself through complete repayment and too frightened to call in the police. Because most loan sharking is conducted by racketeers, borrowers live in fear of harm to themselves or members of their families if they default on payments or reveal the situation to the police.

Assume a poor man has spent his weekly wage drinking and gambling, and has to bring home enough money to purchase groceries for his family. He needs $50. As he voices his problem to the bartender, a man who has been listening sidles over to him and flashes $50. The distressed man takes the money and signs a note to pay back $60, at the rate of $5 a week for twelve weeks. Having to pay $10 in order to borrow $50 does not seem too bad to him, but it works out to an annual true interest rate of about 300 percent. Then suppose the borrower misses a payment. This results in another dollar being added to the principal due. Then when the victim has reduced his debt to $30, the loan shark suggests, "Why not refinance and kick it back to $50?" There is a $2 charge for the refinancing, and the whole procedure starts all over again.

This is obviously no way to borrow money. Even though you may need money desperately, stay away from a loan shark. Becoming involved with one can result in permanent financial disaster for the borrower.

Encouraging the expansion of small-loan companies is the best way to destroy the moneylending business of racketeers. And your best defense against such vultures while they continue to exist is to keep your life insurance cash values in reserve, and to maintain a thrift account or credit union balance sufficient to produce liquid funds to tide you over for at least three months if your income were to be completely cut off. Borrowing out of desperation is undoubtedly the worst possible way; thrift habits can insure you against ever having to take this ruinous course.

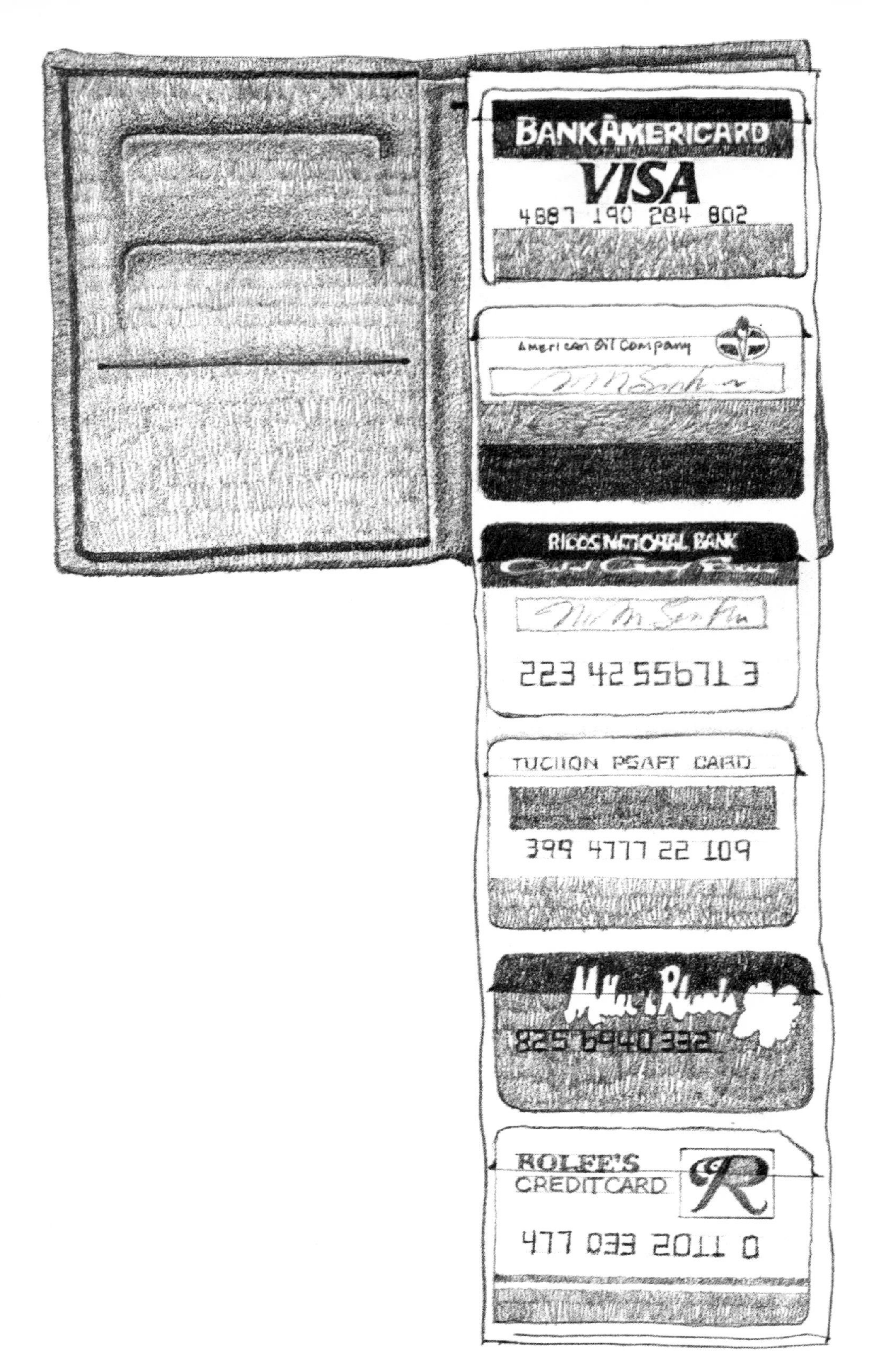
BANKAMERICARD
VISA
4887 190 284 802
American Oil Company
RIGGS NATIONAL BANK
223 42 55671 3
399 4777 22 109
825 6940 332
ROLFE'S
CREDITCARD
477 033 2011 0

CHAPTER 6

Assorted Credit Cards

One of the most remarkable financial instruments ever invented is the credit card. The growth in its acceptance and the business volume it has generated have been phenomenal. In 1975 it was estimated that American consumers held over 370 million credit cards. The approximate number of cards in various categories would be: 140 million, retail store; over 92 million, oil company; 80 million, bank; over 2 million, air travel; over 7 million each in travel, entertainment, and car rental; and over 35 million all-purpose credit cards.

All have as their underlying purpose the stimulation of a substantial increase in sales volume. With a series of cards, you can buy almost anything—from a pocket radio to an ocean cruise; from yoga lessons, weight-watching program, and gold coins to artificial insemination of cattle. Not only humans hold these credit instruments. Some silken cats and petted poodles of the very rich have cards of their own to provide such creature comforts as the services of pet hotels or veterinary clinics.

Credit cards may well be heading us toward a cashless society. Very few people will buy anything but groceries for cash today if they can whip out a card and "sign for it" instead; and this small piece of plastic can instantly deliver an almost infinite variety of goods and services. As a merchandising tool it makes sales where they would be more difficult (or not made at all) if cash were a prerequisite; or where they could be increased in volume if payment were deferred.

Oil company cards

No industrial group has achieved greater mileage from credit cards than the oil companies, which were among the earliest interstate marketers to offer this service. Oil companies now lead all other consumer suppliers, except retail stores, with respect to the number of credit cards in use.

These motoring cards serve four main purposes: for the car owner, they make it unnecessary to carry much cash when traveling, and they consolidate all purchases of gasoline, oil, tires, and accessories on a single monthly bill; for the oil company, they motivate, and tend to assure, customer loyalty to a particular brand of gas or chain of service stations, and they stimulate larger sales and purchase of higher-priced items, because the customer does not have to make a "purse payment." Over $13 billion were charged to motorist credit cards in 1977.

Other advantages of oil company credit include an accurate check on the gas and oil you use; monthly reporting of transportation outlays for expense accounts; and the tabulation of gasoline taxes deductible on your income tax. Of the major oil companies, Mobil has pioneered in marketing general merchandise. It mails out catalogs listing such items as jackets, radios, and stereos, which can be charged to a Mobil credit card.

If you pay your gas and oil charges promptly each month, there is no interest or service charge added. If you are laggard, you will probably be charged interest at the rate of 1½ percent a month on the open balance after sixty days. If you are habitually delinquent in settling your monthly account, your card may be canceled and you will probably find it difficult to obtain another one. There is an American Petroleum Credit Association, a sort of clearinghouse for the industry, and an interchange of information among the leading credit card issuers so that if you establish a reputation for financial unreliability, it will not be a secret.

Abuses reported

In general, motor credit experience has been excellent, with payment defaults amounting over the years to less than 1 percent of total billings. Chronic slow payers may be nursed along, however, because the 1½ percent finance charge compensates for the delay (although that rate was not very rewarding to the issuing company when prime interest rates were 12 percent).

A problem, however, has been fraud and misuse. Losses have been incurred by issuers principally from three causes: (1) cards stolen or misused by a member of the family of the card owner; (2) a card owner who suddenly goes on a purchasing binge; and (3) cards obtained and used by people who make misstatements on their applications and never intend to pay the charges they run up.

Schemes to bilk the oil companies have been legion. One lad charged new tires or batteries at every service station he visited on a trip from New York to Denver.

He would sell the items back to a station attendant or owner for half price, pocket the cash, and go merrily on his way.

Big bills have also been run up through use of stolen cards, sometimes for days before the owners realized and reported their loss. It is essential that if you lose or misplace your credit card, you report this fact to the issuer at once by telegram, telephone, or registered letter, so that the card number may be flashed to all the company's service stations and the card may be canceled.

There is now a federal law limiting your maximum responsibility for charges on stolen credit cards to $50. Further, several states have enacted special legislation to combat card thefts. The toughest law is in Texas, where a conviction for felonious use of a credit card can result in a $10,000 fine and ten years in jail.

Motor credit cards have worked well because the companies have developed a checkup that spots people with bad remittance records and denies cards to them. Also, service attendants can check by phone a master list of stolen and invalidated cards. The interest charges on past-due bills enable companies to be tolerant of dilatory, but essentially honest, customers.

Single-company cards

Other prominent issuers of single-company credit cards are hotel and motel chains, airlines, and national car-rental firms. All of these, quite like department and chain stores, are using credit cards for swift identification and acceptance of individuals who need not pay cash.

Single-company credit cards are created as pipelines to business whereby the cardholder may become almost a "captive" customer. For example, if you have a hotel or motel chain card, you may charge at any of the establishments in the chain. You can also benefit by an advance reservation system assuring you accommodation at the next city or resort you plan to visit. This combined credit and booking service encourages you to favor a given chain exclusively. Holiday Inn, Howard Johnson, Marriott, TraveLodge, Hilton, Western International, and Ramada are among those which encourage the use of their credit cards.

Airlines, too, have millions of their credit cards in use, again making it easy for customers to prefer and to specify a particular line. Capturing traveler loyalty is especially important over highly competitive air routes, such as New York to Miami, New York to Chicago, nonstop coast to coast, and transatlantic flights. A special card issued by the Universal Air Travel Plan permits you to charge airplane trips on any line, but insists that you put down a sizable deposit before the card is issued.

The nationwide car-rental services promote the use of credit cards to develop and retain business in a highly competitive consumer field, to facilitate advance reservations, and to accelerate the pickup and return of rented vehicles. This car-rental business has steadily gravitated to the larger companies, in part because, with a national network of offices, they can arrange for customers to rent a vehicle in one city and return it in another, possibly hundreds of miles away, without any extra charge or penalty.

American Telephone & Telegraph Company allows calls to be charged on its credit cards. At the end of 1977, over 7.6 million of these cards were in use, and billings on them totaled $1 billion for the year. The amount charged averaged about $2.50 per message.

Credit cards are also available which permit you to charge at local stores and restaurants in most cities.

In the past twenty years credit cards have moved from an innovation to an international institution. A problem did develop along the way, however: how to carry a dozen or more credit cards in wallet or pocketbook. Many people acquired accordion-like cases, displaying each card in a plastic see-through compartment. When spread out, this credit card cluster could run as long as two feet. If the carrying case is stolen, the owner has to notify about a dozen different issuers about the loss. Further, the case is uncomfortable to carry in a man's inside or hip pocket.

Another drawback to carrying, and using, so many cards is the number of separate billings coming in each month, creating a complicated set of records for itemizing expense accounts and defining proper cost deductions for income tax purposes. A consolidation of all, or most, of these extensions of credit on one comprehensive credit card would simplify the procedure. This consolidation was accomplished by BankAmericard (now Visa) and Master Charge, and flowered in the three well-known all-purpose cards, American Express, Diners Club, and Carte Blanche, which will be discussed in the following chapter.

Retail store cards

Retail store credit cards, although larger in total number than oil company cards, are more difficult to classify because there is such a diversity of issuers: department stores, retail chains, specialty shops, hardware and garden suppliers, and furniture and appliance specialists.

Cards issued to approved individuals for identification at the point of sale eliminate the need for customer or sales clerk to handle money, assure prompt and accurate recording of transactions, and facilitate computerized accounting. The customer is pleased with the convenience of cashless shopping, and usually is proud to possess and display a credit card as a kind of status symbol. And of course the store is pleased because its sales are significantly expanded by credit extensions;

and possession and use of its card encourages the customer to shop there, rather than patronize a competitor down the street.

Stores formerly "carried" their customers up to sixty days without pressure for payment. In an era of double-digit bank interest rates, however, stores want to receive payments faster. They urge, and indeed specify, remittance by the tenth of the month following billing; and many now send a notice stating that, if the item remains unpaid after thirty days, there will be a carrying charge of from ¾ to 1½ percent per month, depending on state laws and the practice of the particular store. Inflationary conditions in 1973-4 increased the percentage of slow and delinquent accounts, so that interest charges for tardy payments became more essential for profitable store operations.

Related to retail credit cards are various plans to encourage advance or continued shopping. One of these is the lay-away plan. This enables you to select, say, a television set when it is on sale, or an overcoat in August, by paying a small deposit, followed by delivery and billing sixty or ninety days later (usually without any interest or carrying charge on the balance in the interim).

A second service available when charged to your credit card number is the budget plan. This permits you to buy a "big ticket" item for immediate delivery and, at the time of purchase, arrange for the payment to be extended over two to six months' time, paying a stated amount each month and an additional charge, generally between 1 and 1½ percent per month, on the unpaid balance.

An increasingly popular application of store credit cards is the revolving credit account. This operates on the same principle as the revolving credit plan of commercial banks. It establishes an open credit line in the store for approved individuals. Suppose your credit limit is $300; then you can purchase any article or articles not to exceed that amount in total cost. If you buy a television set for $200, it is charged to your account; and you can pay for it over a period of six to twelve months, depending on the store's policy. Up to 1½ percent interest on the unpaid balance will be added monthly, and you still have $100 left for further purchases. You can vary the amount of credit used and the time you take to pay off, always having a buying fund at hand, ranging in amount between zero and $300, depending on the volume of your purchases and the rapidity of your payments.

Use of store credit cards not only makes the money to buy things needed or desired instantly available, but it also helps customers to effect exchanges and adjustments with greater consideration and alacrity. In addition, stores often inform their credit card holders in advance of attractive special values and seasonal sales.

Bank cards

Within the past fifteen years there has emerged a magnified version of the retail store credit card. It is a multiple credit card, which enables you to buy goods on credit from several or even thousands of retailers and have the bills for all of these purchases consolidated on a single monthly statement.

The idea was pioneered by local banks in search of expanded business. They offered to stores in their neighborhood credit availability for their customers, with the banks performing the bookkeeping and the billing. The bank charged each merchant subscribing to the plan a flat percentage (ranging from 2½ to 6 percent) of monthly billings; and was responsible for collection of the accounts.

While the merchants, at the outset, were a little unhappy about giving up a percentage of each credit sale

The Role of Credit Cards In Consumer Debt

(in billions of dollars)

	1965	*1970*	*1971*	*1973*	*1977**
Total	89.9	127.2	138.4	180.5	260.7
Installment	70.9	102.1	111.3	147.4	216.6
Noninstallment	19.0	25.1	27.1	33.0	44.1
Single-payment loans	7.7	9.7	10.6	13.2	15.8
Commercial banks	6.7	8.5	9.3	11.7	13.4
Other financial institutions	1.0	1.2	1.3	1.5	2.4
Charge accounts	6.4	8.0	8.3	9.8	13.5
Retail outlets	5.7	6.2	6.4	7.8	11.1
Credit cards **	0.7	1.8	1.9	2.0	2.4
Service credit ***	4.9	7.4	8.2	10.0	14.8

*Last available statistics for noninstallment credit, December 1977.

**Service station and miscellaneous credit card accounts and home heating oil accounts.

***Debts payable to hospitals, physicians, public utilities, and such.

Sources: Federal Reserve Board, National Consumer Finance Association

to the bank, they were pleased to be able to offer charge accounts to their customers without the burden of billing and collection; and without tying up their capital in accounts receivable. Store owners noted that, as in almost every other retail operation, credit availability expanded total sales.

In the earlier stages of consolidated retail credit, a number of specially created credit service companies, as well as local banks, provided the service. These companies included Charge-A-Plate Group in New York, which gave members the privilege of charging their purchases in any of several well-known stores, such as Bloomingdale's and Arnold Constable and Company; Uni-Service Corporation in Forest Hills, New York; Community Charge Plan in New York; Central Charge Service in Washington, D.C.; and NAC Charge Plan in Baltimore.

Gradually, however, it developed that this sort of combined single-bill credit accommodation could be highly computerized and was a natural for banks; and that a national affiliation seemed desirable so that card-bearing customers might shop not just locally but in major cities and resorts across the land. Thus credit cards broadened their geographical coverage and acquired most of the general attitudes of the all-purpose credit cards.

The business has concentrated under the leadership of major commercial banks; and the dominant consolidated cards in use today are BankAmericard (now Visa), developed by, but no longer controlled by, the largest bank in the United States, Bank of America in Californa, and Master Charge, a similar, competing service sponsored by a large number of metropolitan banks, joined together under Interbank Card Association.

Visa

National BankAmericard, Incorporated (NBI, which has now become Visa USA, Inc.), an independent non-stock membership corporation, was formed in July 1970 to administer, promote, and further develop the BankAmericard (now known as Visa) program throughout the United States. At the end of 1977 the domestic system administered by Visa consisted of 9,709 financial institutions with 31,797 banking offices, serving over 42.6 million cardholders and more than 1,632,000 merchant outlets. Net charge-offs (credit and fraud losses) for 1977 were reported at 1.20 percent of liquidations, up from 1.05 percent in 1974.

Visa bank membership at the end of 1977 consisted of 774 proprietary members and 8,935 agent members. Proprietary members are banking institutions whose primary functions are to issue cards, extend credit to cardholders, provide cardholder services, and solicit new cardholders; develop, maintain, and service contracts with merchants who honor the card; and extend their programs by sponsoring, and entering into, contracts with agent members. Proprietary members have their own names imprinted underneath the Visa name on the cards they use.

Agent members do not issue cards themselves, nor do they extend credit directly to cardholders (although they may participate in the financing of receivables owned by proprietary members). The function of agent members is to develop, maintain, and service contractual relationships with merchants for their proprietary sponsoring members and to assist proprietary members in developing cardholder contracts.

When an individual uses his card to make a purchase from a Visa subscribing merchant, the amount of the sale (minus a small discount) is credited to the merchant's account as soon as he submits the sales draft to his Visa sponsoring bank. The discount, paid by the merchant to the bank, is individually negotiated and varies from 1 to 5 percent. In 1977 the average discount was 2.5 percent.

The total annual transactions run into the billions, and for their recording, billing, and interchange from bank processing center to the card-issuing processing center depend on a network of computers and high-speed communications systems linking the more than eighty Visa processing centers.

Visa holders benefit from: (1) the great number of merchants they can patronize, shopping without check or cash, over a wide geographical range; (2) obtaining cash at over 61,000 domestic and international banking offices; (3) having an average of six weeks to pay without finance charge, providing payment is made in full; and (4) exercise of the option of paying a portion of the balance and extending the remainder (paying a finance charge subject to state regulations).

There is no yearly subscription charge made for

Visa, with a few isolated exceptions. The average billings per individual statement during 1977 were $81.22 per month.

Although Visa was a pioneer in the development of bank credit cards and became the first all-purpose bank card to be accepted throughout the United States, it does not have the field entirely to itself. The other major national bank card system, Master Charge, shares with Visa the almost total coverage of bank credit card issuance and use.

Master Charge

Master Charge is the service mark used by more than 7,000 banks in the United States that participate in the program licensed and sponsored by Interbank Card Association. Master Charge has moved rapidly forward, implementing, with Visa, dramatic and important changes in consumer credit, personal money management, retail merchandising, and operating procedures in the banking industry.

For 1977 the Interbank group of Master Charge card licensees posted an annual dollar volume of $16.7 billion. Master Charge on that date had 47.7 million individual cardholders and 19.6 million active accounts. These active accounts are used about twice a month; and the average outstanding balance per active account was $406.69. The average cash advance was $112.63 and the average transaction was $27.89.

Interbank Card Association, headquartered in New York City, is a nonprofit corporation established in 1966 to promote and facilitate the national and international use of the Interbank/Master Charge card.

As with other bank cards, Master Charge makes it possible for bank customers to charge purchases not only at local merchant establishments but at those across the nation affiliated with that particular bank card. There is no cost for this service if the cardholder pays his entire bill within the period specified by the bank, generally twenty-five days. At the cardholder's option, he may repay part of his unpaid balance and put the rest into a revolving, or deferred, payment account, for which a service or interest charge is made on the unpaid balance. The cardholder can not only charge; he or she can borrow cash up to an individual credit limit determined by the bank.

Master Charge cards are accepted by thousands of professional service accounts such as hospitals, doctors, dentists, and veterinarians.

Master Charge created its national interchange system as an arrangement in which all banks issuing Master Charge cards agree to have their affiliated merchants honor the cards of all other banks in the system, and exchange sales drafts with each other. This interchange greatly broadens the range of acceptance of bank cards and, indeed, has become international in scope. Master Charge is now accepted in Canada and Mexico, and by many banks in the countries of Europe, Central and South America, the Caribbean islands, Hong Kong, Tahiti, Thailand, and the Philippines. Cash can be secured abroad via Master Charge in some 3,000 financial offices.

Interbank Card Association has become the largest bank card network in the world, an organization that in 1977 accounted for transactions totaling more than $16.7 billion.

Use of the Master Charge card is simple. The customer presents his card to the merchant, who examines it to see that it has not expired and is not on a "restricted" list. Purchases are generally limited to the merchant's "floor release limit" (a transaction of a size that does not require authorization). The merchant sends the sales slip to his Master Charge bank and receives immediate credit for its full amount. The merchant's bank processes the sales slips and sends them to the cardholder's bank which issued the card and which bills the customer each month. The merchant's bank uses an Interbank draft on the cardholder's bank to settle the day's transaction.

Authorization for acceptance of transactions above standard limits is obtained by the merchant by contacting an authorization center of Interbank National of Interbank Card Association. INAS is now to be improved by complete use of descriptive billing, whereby cardholders receive information about their purchases on a statement, rather than receiving copies of their original receipts. This will reduce costs and eliminate the transfer of sales slips from the acquiring bank to the issuing bank and finally to the cardholder.

Electronic transfer of descriptive billing is the next step preceding an International Network for Electronic Transfer (INET), scheduled to become a new feature of Master Charge. INET would make it possible to obtain cash, make purchases, guarantee checks, or transfer funds from one account to another through instantaneous access to checking or savings accounts. International electronic transfer of funds would greatly reduce the number of checks people write, provide instant funds for banks (instead of waiting for checks to clear), and give merchants assurance that checks would not bounce. According to the Federal Reserve Bank, 300,000 checks on banks in the United States are returned each day for a variety of reasons, including insufficient funds.

Bank cards fill needs

The bank charge card answers the need of individual banks for a modern extremely rapid instrument of exchange and the need of customers for a convenient cashless way to purchase goods or services and pay for them over a period of time. The charge privilege, once confined specifically to patrons of a single business establishment, is now becoming almost universal. In this revolutionary transition, bank cards are playing a major role. They expand the sales of merchants by providing screened credit, and by assuming all the costs and details of billing and collection. In doing this the subscribing banks gain the average of 3 to 5 percent discounts and earn substantial amounts of interest on delayed payments and revolving credits. Further, in a world made increasingly risky by muggings, holdups, and frauds, cardholding individuals benefit greatly because they no longer need to carry large amounts of cash with them.

Bank cards—Master Charge and Visa—are making significant inroads on the "all-purpose card" primarily intended to provide credit for travel and entertainment. Bank cards make no annual charge to their customers; travel and entertainment cards do. Bank cards have a built-in system for purchase of virtually everything by means of extended payments and allow twenty-five days for payment on open billings.

Credit cards represent the flowering competence of computers and electronic communication. There is no visible end to the issuance and application of these cards; and the bank card may become increasingly the most ascendant variety.

CHAPTER 7

All-Purpose Credit Cards

While credit cards of all types were designed to expand business volume, some of the big individual issuers—airlines, motel chains, oil companies—have become concerned that their share of the market is being taken away from them by the bank cards and the all-purpose cards.

When oil companies began issuing credit cards, they sought to build customer loyalty to their particular brands. Each company wanted motorists to defer stopping for gas along the road until they came to a station honoring its card—Shell, Exxon, Sun, Texaco, Mobil, Getty, and others. Now that a credit card is honored at the pumps of dozens of different oil companies, the earlier insistence of the customer on a particular brand has diminished; and credit cards now tend to retain customer loyalty to one brand principally at neighborhood stations and less on the open road.

It is clear that the big swing today is toward the more inclusive cards: bank cards and all-purpose cards, a field now divided up among three global competitors—American Express, Diners Club, and Carte Blanche. These companies devised a dual approach to profitability: they charge annual fees for membership; and they also collect a discount from subscribing retailers who honor the cards. The idea of commanding patronage for a specific store, restaurant, motel chain, or airline does not apply. Instead, the all-purpose issuers stress the universality of their cards; the myriads of goods and services from innumerable retailers these cards make available in many lands; and the instant emergency cash they can procure in Calcutta, Chicago, or Cologne. Reading the advertisements of these marketers of financial magic carpets is like receiving an engraved invitation from Marco Polo.

Here is a composite distillation of the alluring inducements of credit card membership. "Our card is almost a necessity in today's world. If you stay at home you can 'fill 'er up' at any of a dozen nearby service stations, instantly open a charge account in the best stores in town, dine at the finest restaurants, stay at a motel, or buy a gift for a friend, flowers for an invalid, take reducing lessons, or join a book club."

If travel is your wish, your all-purpose card is your financial passport to a flight to Europe, a casino-hotel in Las Vegas, skiing in Colorado, fishing in Canada, golfing in Scotland, sunning in Miami, Aruba, Nice, or Acapulco, renting a car or a camel, or entertaining friends at the "Top of the Mark."

The credit available is, of course, not infinite but most all-purpose cards are flexible within a limit on total current charges up to $500; and the executive card of American Express extends to the ultra credit-worthy a much higher ceiling.

All issuers require an annual membership fee, history of personal integrity and solvency; and immediate payment of regular monthly bills when received. All list your purchases, wherever made, on a single monthly statement, carefully documenting your personal and business expenses.

The all-purpose card is your letter of introduction and your personal credit reference around the world. As a convenience, as a financial protection limiting the carrying of cash to a minimum, and as a badge of status, there is nothing like an international credit card. If the card is lost or stolen, you are protected (but expected to report the loss as soon as possible) ; and your maximum liability in such event is limited to $50.

Diners Club

Of the three major international credit cards available, Diners Club was the pioneer in the field. It claims to be honored at many thousands more places around the world than any other executive credit card.

The Diners Club concept was originated by Frank MacNamara. He got the idea of a credit card, in 1950, after he had dined in a New York restaurant, found that he did not have his wallet with him, and had to wait at the restaurant until his wife could come in from a suburb with the money to pay the check. MacNamara joined forces with Ralph Schneider to form the Diners Club.

At first they solicited restaurants, persuading several to subscribe to the system whereby their patrons got credit privileges and were billed by Diners Club, not by the restaurant. Diners Club deducted 7 percent of the total restaurant bill (including taxes and tips) for its services in credit investigation, accounting, and collection; and it encouraged its club members to patronize restaurants honoring its card.

It took a while for the idea to catch on, but the status of having a comprehensive credit card, and the convenience of having a single organization render a combined monthly bill, to be paid by a single check, proved highly attractive. Getting retailers in cities across the country to subscribe required a major sales effort; and credit criteria needed to be established for club members in order to make sure that only those who had the resources and the disposition to pay promptly were enrolled.

Gradually corporations accepted the idea of having the expense accounts of their executives and salesmen itemized uniformly. (Salesmen and executives probably comprise the largest categories of Diners Club members.) The original $5 annual membership fee has been increased to $20, with *Diners Club Magazine* costing $4 extra. The 7 percent charge, originally levied on restaurant business, has become an average of about 4½ percent, depending on the type of retail establishment and other factors.

The financial success of Diners Club was swift and sensational. MacNamara sold out early to Schneider, who became board chairman, with Alfred Bloomingdale as president. In 1960, total billings crossed the $160 million level, and company earnings in that year were close to $2 million.

In May 1975, Diners Club had over 3.3 million credit cards in the Diners Club family, and over 400,000 firms worldwide honored its cards. In addition to traditional retailers, about thirty-five coin dealers had been added to accommodate the rapidly growing number of people —believed to total 9 million Americans—who collect gold and silver coins. The average annual total of charges run up by Diners Club cardholders is now more than $600. Regular monthly bills must be paid at once; but for large items—airline tickets, tours, and such—financing can be arranged at a 12 percent annual interest rate. Diners Club also provides $30,000 of travel accident insurance on airline tickets charged to its card and has a $25,000 Executive Credit plan.

Diners Club, the pioneer in universal cards did much to change people's financial philosophy. It has become unfashionable to pay cash. Thrift once was regarded as the cardinal financial virtue; now the ability to spend substantially seems to be more revered. Credit in general and all-purpose cards in particular provide the instant gratification sought by believers in an "enjoy now, pay later" philosophy. So far it has all worked out well, with only a small percentage of Americans getting into debt over their heads.

American Express

Because of its renowned travel facilities and the use of its travelers' checks all over the world for decades, it was quite logical for American Express to enter the credit card business. The American Express card was introduced in 1958. It was well promoted, caught on rapidly, and now is a major all-purpose card.

Initially, there were about 240,000 American Express card holders and 17,500 service establishments honoring the card. Six months later, the 1958 annual report of American Express Company revealed that there were more than 600,000 cardholders enjoying American Express credit service at 32,000 establishments in seventy-two countries.

Requirements for enrollment in American Express at that time were set several notches higher than for the general run of merchandise credit or bank cards. To be a member, you had to evidence a satisfactory credit history and a dependable income of $7,500 or more. Credit investigations were quite thorough, because the cards would be used all over the world, and a significant percentage of defaulters could torpedo the enterprise. Special consideration was given to college graduates who had been accepted for employment by reputable companies, even though such persons were too young to have a history of satisfactory credit.

Because of its travel orientation, American Express began to sign up regional airlines. In March, 1964, American Airlines entered the fold, and other major airlines followed suit in due course. This penetration of the air transportation field led to the American Express "sign and fly" plan, promoted in 1964; and today American Express cardholders can charge flights on 160 airlines in all parts of the world.

The variety of features and facilities offered to American Express cardholders has been steadily expanded. In 1963, an all-accident insurance policy was made available; in 1964, term life insurance policies were added. Also in 1964, the card was introduced in four foreign currencies in addition to American and Canadian dollars: the Mexican peso, French franc, German mark, and English pound sterling. A number of other currencies have been added since.

In 1965, American Express signed with major railroad and steamship lines and ski resorts; and made its worldwide program of escorted tours available on an extended-payment plan. In that same year the company pioneered with a $100 deductible liability protection plan, whereby the cardholder was protected against all liability if he notified the company before use of the card by an illegal possessor. If he failed to notify the company, his maximum liability was limited to $100. (The limit has since been reduced to $50.)

Noting the rapid expansion of bank credit cards, American Express in 1966 introduced its own elite version, the unique bank executive credit card plan, available to all banks without the payment of any franchise or license fee. Participating banks offer the "Gold Card," jointly sponsored by the bank and American Express, extending a $2,000 line of bank credit to carefully selected individuals, along with all the standard privileges of the American Express card. This executive card enables the holder to draw on his credit for the purchase of American Express travelers' checks, with a limit of $500 in the United States and $1,000 overseas; and to cash personal checks, providing that proceeds, above $50 in cash, be used to purchase American Express travelers' checks, up to a $500 limit overseas.

Other innovations in the use of these credit cards include a $100,000 flight protection plan costing only $3 a trip, and "Be My Guest," which allows cardholders to be remote hosts, treating friends to dinner, simply by telephoning a restaurant anywhere in the world. American Express cards also allow you to get cash at airports, and they provide credit at more than 145 medical centers.

In 1967, American Express inaugurated its Superphone system, enabling service establishments to telephone free of charge from anywhere in the United States to the New York authorization unit to check on the validity of any American Express money card.

American Express and other all-purpose cards are known as "T and E" cards, because they are primarily used for travel and entertainment.

A study by American Express in 1977 indicated that over 85 percent of its cardholders used their membership for hotel/motel accommodations; 80 percent for restaurants; and 60 percent for airlines. The lesser uses were car rentals, retail stores, and gas stations. A profile of the typical cardholder is: age thirty-five or older, a professional or manager earning above $20,000 annually, and a college graduate.

Today, there are more than 8.6 million American Express credit card users, and some 250,000 establishments around the world honor the card. The annual membership fee is $20 for the regular card and $30 for the gold card with its special privileges. Cards for other members of the family cost $10 each, with no limit on the number of supplementary cards which may be obtained. Membership includes the magazine, *Travel and Leisure*.

American Express indicates that the average purchase is approximately $100 and that, generally, the cardholder spends 56 percent more than the person who uses a retail store credit card, and up to four times more than the amount of the average cash transaction. Defaulting cardholders are believed to be less than 1 percent.

The discounts received by American Express from retailers, transportation companies, and service establishments range between 3 and 6 percent, depending on the type and volume of business done. Airline discounts are lower than those of restaurants because of the far greater dollar volume of flight ticket purchases.

To handle its huge business volume, to process new account applications, to pay service establishments, and to bill and collect from cardholders, American Express operations are highly computerized. These procedures are concentrated in five regional centers: Phoenix, New York City, Miami, Mexico City, and Haywards Heath, just outside of London.

Carte Blanche

This member of the big three in all-purpose, or T and E, cards is a subsidiary of Avco Corporation, a diversified holding company whose shares are listed on the New York Stock Exchange.

At the end of 1977, Carte Blanche cardholders numbered nearly 731,000 and its cards were honored at over 255,000 establishments in the United States, Canada, and overseas.

For fiscal 1977, Carte Blanche reported total revenues of more than $30.2 million derived from membership fees, discounts, travel income, services, and other charges. This compares with $29.6 million reported in 1973. Discounts vary from 3 to 10 percent depending on the type of business.

Beginning in September 1974, the annual membership fee for Carte Blanche cardholders became $20, which included $2.50 for a yearly subscription to *Carte Blanche Magazine,* dealing with travel and entertainment. Supplementary cards for family members cost $10 per year for each additional card.

Other features of Carte Blanche include these services, which were introduced in 1973: ready-cash loans, enabling cardholders to borrow up to $500 at any of the 1,400 Avco Financial service offices in the United States and Canada; and executive loan-by-mail programs whereby Carte Blanche members may borrow $1,500 to $5,000 by mail with extended payment plans available. Additional special Carte Blanche services include guaranteed admission credit at hundreds of selected hospitals and Intermedic, which entitles members to the services of English-speaking doctors in seventy-five countries.

For those laggard in settling their Carte Blanche billings there is a late charge equal to 1½ percent of the unpaid balance assessed after sixty days' delinquency. There are also delayed-payment plans, with interest levied, for charges involving airline tickets; and four- to twelve-month payment plans relating to various merchandise offers.

Carte Blanche does not make public the average monthly or annual charges run up by its members, nor information regarding delinquency of its cardholders or terminations of membership for that reason.

The company has been aggressive in extending its franchises internationally and now has franchises in

DINERS
CLUB
VISA
OPEN DAILY

Australia, India, Iran, Italy, Japan, Lebanon, Malaysia, New Zealand, Thailand, and Venezuela.

Carte Blanche, together with American Express and Diners Club, is energetically broadening the global acceptance of T and E cards.

Profits and losses

While the issuance of credit cards by gasoline retailers, car-rental companies, department stores, motels, and airlines is designed primarily as a sales tool to expand a company's business, the bank cards and the all-purpose cards are intended to generate profits for those issuing them. Among the three big issuers of all-purpose cards, Diners Club profited for eighteen years but then showed heavy losses in the period of economic decline during 1969-70. Part of this loss was due to unprofitable entry into a travel agency franchise and an international hotel reservation business by acquisitions.

Payment delinquencies of ninety days or more for Diners Club members were reported to have doubled between mid-1969 and the end of 1970. The stock market decline eroded the discretionary incomes of hundreds of thousands of persons, and hitherto free-spenders had to tighten their belts. Also, thousands lost their jobs, and payments on credit card accounts were an early casualty, coming generally at the end of family budget allocations. Carte Blanche, too, reported operating deficits in this period (over $2.5 million in an eighteen-month period ending in June, 1971). American Express also experienced an increase in its delinquent accounts during that recession. Its long-run operations, however, are believed to have been substantially profitable, although specific earnings from its credit card operation have not been shown separately in its earnings statements. Unlike the banks, all-purpose card issuers make little revenue on interest. Installment purchases form only a small part of total credit volume; and interest charged usually at 1 percent a month on past-due accounts is not a significant part of gross revenues.

Combating frauds

In common with all other issuers, the T and E card distributors need always to be on the alert to minimize their losses. A rather sizable list of people, unacceptable on the basis of past credit records, has been compiled; and formerly prompt payers who develop delinquent habits are swiftly eliminated.

Frauds have been reduced, first by better screening at the time of issuance. A serious problem had been the snatching of new credit cards from the mailboxes of subscribers. The thief signed the registered subscriber's name on the card and used it to buy heavily until the issuer caught up with him. Favorite fraudulent purchases are such readily salable items as radios, television sets, cameras, and airline tickets.

To defend against such larceny, American Express developed a dual-dating procedure, mailing out the credit card, and then, some days later, a letter asking if the card had been received.

The best defense against fraud, however, seems to be the card with the owner's picture on it. Banks that have adopted this procedure have found it effective because a thief is unlikely to risk visual comparison of his profile with the picture of the true owner on the card.

When a credit card is put to fraudulent use, the telltale evidence is overactivity. This is picked up by computers, and whenever unusually large amounts are charged against a card or an excess of purchase activity appears, the computer "kicks out" the card; the credit department is instantly notified; and someone contacts the cardholder, asking, "Did you make all those purchases?" "Have you lost your card?" Further defensive measures relate to "limit" buying. If a cardholder enters a store and his intended purchase exceeds the "floor release limit" of the establishment, the sales clerk can telephone the issuer's nearest authorization center for instruction on whether to allow purchase of the merchandise.

It appears that the fraud element has now been placed under better control. Credit problems, however, can still arise during a recession when people, normally financially dependable, get into a bind, or lose their jobs, or are on strike. Also, on occasion, cardholders go on credit sprees and acquire more goods and services than they can pay for conveniently or currently. There was some concern about an increase in this impulsive buying when double-digit inflation occurred in 1974, creating an attitude of "buy today because it will cost more tomorrow." Indeed, the darkest cloud on the credit card horizon may be this deterioration of individual credit in an inflationary economy. In 1974 there was noted a significant rise in the percentage of consumers delinquent in installment purchase contracts. With lower inflation in 1975 and 1976 the percentage of these delinquent consumers declined.

Discounts for cash customers

The latest problem for the all-purpose card issuers has arisen as a result of legal action brought by Consumers Union against American Express, charging that the company forbade those merchants who honored its credit card to offer or allow discounts to cash customers. Subscribing merchants who contract to honor "plastic money" customarily accord a discount of from 2 to 8 percent of their credit card sales to the issuing companies. This discount is, of course, added onto or included in the retail price of merchandise or the cost of a meal in a restaurant. Cash customers obviously derive no benefit from this credit payment system, but rather subsidize the arrangement because they have to pay the higher prices which include the cost of credit. Consumers Union contended that those who pay cash are entitled to a lower price.

American Express denied that it was at fault but did agree to an out-of-court settlement, and to send notices to about 87,000 subscribing merchants that they might, if they chose, offer discounts to cash customers. The merchants are under no obligation to do so, but a merchant who does allow a discount for cash must offer it "clearly and conspicuously" to everyone.

Many subscribing merchants may not go along with such a two-tier price system because of the accounting complications that may result. Whether service establishments will make cash discounts a regular practice depends, apparently, on how vocal or insistent the consumer demand is. The cash discount does not provide the regular monthly billing and itemized record of expenditures now traditional with plastic money. Besides, customers have become accustomed to buying on credit, and to spending 20 or 30 percent more at a restaurant or retail shop because they do not have to pay the bill immediately in cash.

The Consumers Union action may create a precedent for corresponding procedures by other credit dispensers, principally the bank card issuers who also have established discount arrangements with cooperating merchants. Banks have, however, a sizable source of earnings that the T and E issuers lack: namely, interest, which may run as high as 1½ percent per month on cash advances.

Big three compete

There exists a lively competition among the three major T and E card issuers. For various reasons, subscribing service establishments may change their allegiances, dropping one card service and taking on another; and each issuer makes much of the fact when its credit card is accepted where another may not be. This competition for merchant patronage has led to certain reductions in discounts in various retail categories, and, of course, the merchant is eager to keep his discount payments to a minimum.

In any event, the long-range outlook for T and E cards appears excellent and, assuming a continuing inflation and barring an extended depression, total volume of annual billings in this credit category may reach $10 billion by 1980.

These T and E cards, together with all other credit cards, are developments in what is probably a steady progression toward a cashless society. Banks, burdened by the handling of trillions of checks each year, will welcome a system that reduces monthly payments by individuals to one or two checks covering all goods and services they acquire.

It seems possible that not only expenditures for food, apparel, education, and leisure can be consolidated, but also individual debits for interest and payments on loans and mortgages or for rent, payments for life insurance or securities, and deposits in savings accounts and in pension funds could all be grouped together, itemized, and handled each month, merely by budgeted payments to a single credit and disbursing agency via a supercredit card. The owner of such a card would have his creditworthiness thoroughly documented, and would be able at any time to buy or borrow within prescribed limits without any need to present a number of credentials or to draw up a current balance sheet. Such perhaps is the "omnicard" of the future.

CHAPTER 8

Retail Credit

America is a nation of consumers, and we spend about 94 cents of each after-tax dollar, allocating the rest to various forms of thrift and investment. This was the picture in mid-1977, with spending technically divided into two compartments—cash and credit. The money we spend for food, except in restaurants and hotels, is almost entirely in cash. The supermarket, the delicatessen, and fast-food operations all require payment in cash. Other small but regular purchases—public transportation fares, newspapers, candy, gum, cigarettes, a beer at your neighborhood bar or a fifth at the package store —are also cash items.

A number of other common outlays involve short-term credit, with little or no investigation as to your solvency by the creditor. You are billed monthly for club

Personal Income and Expenditure

Distribution of the Personal Income Dollar, 1977

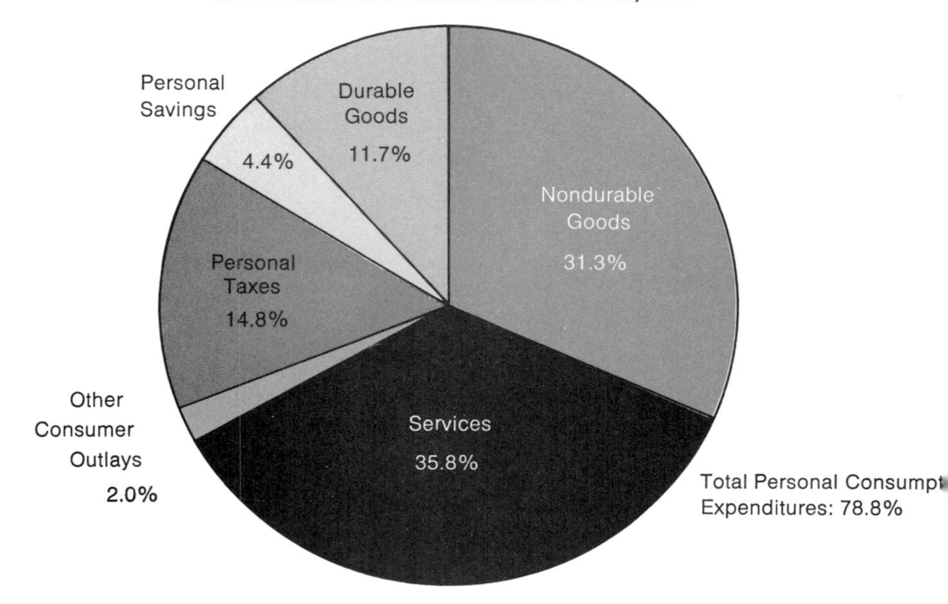

Distribution of Personal Consumption Expenditures, 1977

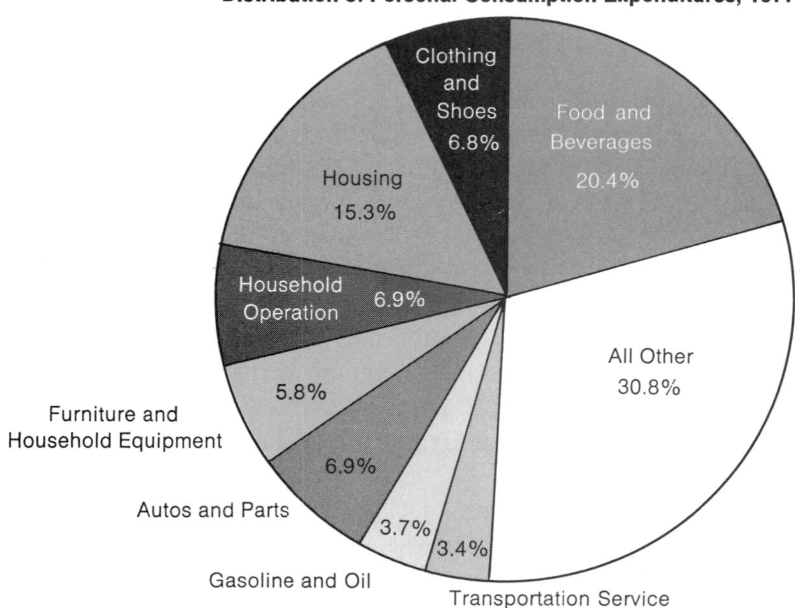

Sources: U.S. Department of Commerce, National Consumer Finance Association

dues; gas, electric, and telephone services; and for the services of physicians or dentists in the month after you have availed yourself of their talents. These extensions of credit are almost automatic; and they are always available to you, without any interest or service charge, unless you are a very slow payer, or an outright deadbeat. These are strictly courtesy or convenience credits.

Department store charge accounts

Most purchases you make at a department store are charged, and billed at the end of each month; and paid for on or before a set date of the next month without interest penalty.

The traditional department store charge account generally was adequate to cover consumer needs when just shoes, clothing, yard goods, curtains, and linens were purchased; but when big-ticket items—furniture, refrigerators, television sets, kitchen ranges, and fur coats —became widely offered, new payment methods had to be developed, because most people did not have sufficient liquid resources to pay cash immediately, or even within forty-five days, for expensive goods.

So, after observing the success of automobile companies in selling on a long-term installment basis and collecting interest on balances, department stores evolved their own credit techniques. They became less patient with monthly charge account stragglers. They sent notices, telephoned laggard customers, and threatened to cancel charge accounts (and not infrequently did) in order to receive payments within a reasonable time period. The open credit account is still a major factor in department store merchandising, made more profitable now by the quite general practice of charging 1 or 1½ percent per month interest on unpaid balances after thirty to sixty days.

However, to stimulate purchases of expensive items

and to encourage more frequent shopping, department stores designed plans for purchase on an installment basis, so that families became accustomed to allocating a certain amount of their budgets each month for department store purchases, in the same way that they allocated monthly quotas for food, rent, insurance, and other items. Not only was this credit enlargement good business in that it expanded sales, but stores found that there were windfall profits to be gleaned from interest charges, and that people were less price-conscious when they did not have to pay cash immediately. Also, goods sold on the installment plan often carry the highest profit margins.

Three types of store credit

There are, today, three types of credit in general use in mass merchandising by department and chain stores. The first is the familiar charge account, for which billings are totaled at the month's end and customarily paid on or before a specified date of the following month, without any interest charge or penalty. This type of charge account has now been modified by many major merchants, so that the customer, if he or she so desires, may pay as little as one-fifth of the month-end billing, and extend the balance by payment of an interest charge on it, calculated at the rate of 12 or 18 percent a year, depending on state laws. However, any time he or she wishes, the customer may pay the balance in full and stop the accrual of interest. This system of paying about one-fifth and extending the balance each month can be continued indefinitely.

The second widely used store-credit arrangement is designed to accommodate more expensive purchases and debit balances. It is variously known as a revolving credit, or a continuous budget payment, account. Under this plan, the customer is given (after some investiga-

Standard Costs of Major Items Purchased by Installment Payments

(based on New York State interest laws)

A $400 Electric Refrigerator

Purchase price	$400.00
Down payment	none required
Balance	400.00
Finance charge	51.92
Total note	451.92
24-month contract	18.83 monthly payment
True interest rate	12% annualized

A $600 Sofa

Purchase price	$600.00
Down payment	none required
Balance	600.00
Finance charge	78.00
Total note	678.00
24-month contract	28.25 monthly payment
True interest rate	12% annualized

A $3,000 Travel Trailer

Purchase price	$3,000.00
Down payment	450.00
Balance	2,550.00
Finance charge	264.00
Total note	3,264.00
48-month contract	68.00 monthly payment
True interest rate	12.68% annualized

A $9,000 Mobile Home

Purchase price	$9,000.00
Down payment	1,350.00
Balance	7,650.00
Finance charge	5,354.00
Total note	13,004.00
120-month contract	108.37 monthly payment
True interest rate	11.69% annualized

A $10,000 Motor Home

Purchase price	$10,000.00
Down payment	2,000.00
Balance	8,000.00
Finance charge	3,330.16
Total note	13,360.16
72-month contract	157.78 monthly payment
True interest rate	12.33% annualized

tion as to his credit-worthiness) a limit, most commonly $500. The customer is privileged to make purchases up to that limit at any time, but is expected to make payments of approximately 5 percent on the open balance of the preceding billing period, and to pay interest at specified rates (12 to 18 percent) on the previous balance without deducting any payments or other credits and without adding current purchases. This revolving credit is similar to the type used for repaying cash loans at commercial banks.

The third credit form is the time-payment or installment plan, and is generally used on big-ticket merchandise such as furniture, pianos, power lawn mowers, outboard motor boats, refrigerators, and other expensive appliances. In practice, credit extended under this type of credit runs above the standard $500 revolving credit limit; and payment may be spaced out for as long as thirty-six months. In such installment or time-payment plans, the customer must be fully and accurately informed as to: (1) the delivered price of the merchandise, including taxes and installation charges, if any; (2) the total amount of interest or service charge added on; (3) the precise amounts of monthly payments; and (4) the true annual interest rate assessed for extended payment.

These three basic types of store credit extensions may be variously geared to, or displaced by, the credit cards of each store chain, or bank cards such as Visa and Master Charge.

Credit in the retail business is ultimately based on two qualifications: ability to pay and willingness to do so. With proper assurance on these points, stores have prospered on credit business.

By way of illustration and example, the J.C. Penney Company reported total sales in 1976 of $8.354 billion, of which $3.1 billion were on credit. This represented 40.3 percent of sales, up from 38.7 percent in 1972. Of this entire credit volume, 86 percent was on regular charge accounts; and 14 percent on time-payment accounts, with true interest varying between 12 and 18 percent, depending on the laws of the states in which stores are located. Active regular charge accounts at the end of 1976 totaled 10.1 million, and time accounts, 1.3 million. J.C. Penney honors its own credit cards, and does not welcome payment by means of Visa or Master Charge.

J.C. Penney, a highly successful merchant chain, is generally regarded as a representative retail company. The firm's credit policies must be sound because their allowance for uncollected accounts was below 2 percent in 1976.

Teen-age credit

Although credit is a nationwide phenomenon, we tend to think of it as an adult privilege. Actually a great deal of credit is extended to, and used by, teen-agers for several years before they complete their educations or establish their own homes. A study prepared by the W.R. Simmons Company of New York showed the following use of credit by youngsters in forty-eight states interviewed in 1970:

	Boys	*Girls*
	(Aged 10 to 17)	
Total in age group	16,178,000	15,608,000
Gas credit cards	772,000	462,000
Department store cards	825,000	1,418,000
BankAmericard (now Visa)	215,000	184,184
Master Charge	232,000	87,000

(Syndicated study *Selected Markets and Media Reaching Them*, 1971)

These credit cards are either in the youngsters' own names, or in the names of adult members of their families. Most of these cards are probably parent-owned, as laws in many states would not permit the collection of debts from persons who are not adults—ruling out in most cases those who are under eighteen.

Actually there has been considerable encouragement given to teen-agers to borrow in order to buy. Banks and merchants who have done pioneer work in this field claim that the earning power and the dependability of payment by teen-agers have been satisfactory. These sources of credit also state that the practical education of youngsters in handling credit is useful and that establishing a sound credit rating at an early age, and learning to gear debt to income and resources are socially constructive, reliance on credit having become an integral part of our way of life. Further, lenders say that in making credit available to juveniles they are building long-term goodwill for their organization. (One youth, as an example, was granted a gas credit card by Mobil but not by other oil companies while he was in college. He still gives Mobil priority on all his gas purchases, and he now owns two cars.)

It is estimated that American teen-age boys and girls now earn over $24 billion annually, so they have, indeed, a considerable capacity to pay for purchases.

Department stores and banks consider teen-agers credit-worthy, especially if they are eighteen or older. Department stores in several cities have experimented with extending credit to those as young as thirteen, particularly if the youngsters had part-time jobs. Credit limits were generally set between $15 and $100; and children felt very important when asked to fill out a credit questionnaire. Sometimes revolving credits up to a limit of $150 were arranged; and youngsters, for the first time, realized that interest charges might run as high as 18 percent annually. For many, this was an eye-opener.

In allowing younger children to obtain credit for purchases, merchants placed emphasis on the solvency and the credit-worthiness of the parents. However, with women attaining their majority in many states at eighteen, accounts in their own names have become quite standard; and of course the hundreds of thousands of teen-age marriages (creating an early need for funds to furnish homes) have been responsible for a big upsurge in the percentage of consumer loan accounts at department stores with debtors below age twenty-one.

In general this teen-age apprenticeship has been well served. If youngsters became overextended and had to run to parents for help, the parental disciplining and reproach made its mark and so led to better credit habits in future.

Opponents of teen-age credit have been numerous and vocal. Economists and educators have suggested that home life has already been made tense for many by family credit problems, and that children should be brought up to eschew credit rather than embrace it. These exponents of the earlier American emphasis on thrift and the avoidance of debt may have a point. Certainly inflation would be far less a problem if everyone paid cash for everything.

CHAPTER 9

Automobile Credit

America's love affair with the automobile is well known. There are now over 105 million passenger cars on our highways, and the frequent shopping for, and possession of, the latest model has been a perennial family ritual for several decades.

A new car, particularly one of the prestige models, has represented for decades a significant status symbol in the American social system. Millions of people lay out more total capital for the purchase of cars in their lifetimes than for their investments in home ownership. An important part of all that automotive outlay is the cost of credit.

It is unusual to buy a car for cash in America. This is mainly because most people simply do not have conveniently available the amount of cash required for outright purchase. They have to struggle to make even a 25 percent down payment, and in any case, most new cars are purchased by trading in a used car to provide at least part of the down payment. More than 70 percent of all new cars and an even higher percentage of used cars are bought "on time"; and over two-thirds of these are acquired on installment contracts running for thirty-six months. This three-year contract has become a standard because, if the credit period ran longer, the amount owed on the car might be more than the vehicle would bring if sold, and the owner might then default, and let his car be repossessed, rather than complete the payments.

The history of mass motor car selling shows steadily rising car prices, lengthened installment purchase periods, lower down payments, and finance charges increasing year by year. These charges have risen because of the first three factors mentioned; and also because since 1969 interest rates have gone wild. To illustrate, the prime bank rate was 8½ percent in July 1969 and 12¼ percent in July 1974. This prime rate exerts a pervasive influence on all interest charges. In March 1977 the prime rate was 7 percent and motor car loans in New York banks averaged about 12.25 percent for financing.

Autos lead consumer debts

The mania for car ownership in America and the fact that only one family out of five in the country has liquid assets of $2,500 have together made autos the leading item in the consumer installment debt categories. Henry Ford set the economic stage for mass buying of motor cars when he established a $5-a-day minimum wage scale at his Detroit factory in 1913. That rate attracted national attention and stimulated demand for higher incomes for industrial workers across the land.

The second event that brought cars within the reach

of the average man was the evolution of debt merchandising in the automobile industry. In early days cars were not expensive, by modern standards. The factory price for cars in 1914 averaged about $775. However, even that amount was higher than industrial wages, which averaged at the time about $625 a year. Then in 1915 along came the Commercial Credit Company—now one of the leading sales finance firms in the country—with an acceptable car purchase installment plan. The original contract called for 50 percent down (later reduced to 40 percent) with the balance payable over eight months.

In the 1920s the payment period began to stretch: first to a one-year contract; then to two years by 1948; thirty months in the 1950s; and now three years. Along the way, as lenders gained experience with this kind of credit and learned that repossessed cars could be readily sold, down payments were gradually reduced to one-third of the purchase price; then to 25 percent; and in 1970 you could buy a car with a 20 percent down payment. (In 1977 new car loans were available with nothing down and forty-eight months to pay.)

While this credit progression seemed natural and logical enough as per capita incomes steadily rose (along with the delivered prices of cars), the rate of increase in the required monthly payment was a bit startling. Monthly payment on a lower-priced car bought in 1955, at a delivered price of $2,900 with 40 percent down payment and twenty-four-month contract, came to about $75. Later comparisons are confusing because of higher prices, lower down payments, and longer installment periods. In 1975 the average monthly payment on car contracts was about $130, not including casualty insurance. There are requirements in almost all contracts for carrying sufficient car insurance. Declining-balance term life insurance on the buyer is customary. Most people prefer to obtain their casualty insurance elsewhere, but in any event evidence of such insurance in force must be given to the sales finance company before the credit extension is approved.

Car credit different

Automobile credit differs from all the other types of consumer credit. First, the manufacturer is paid for each car before it is delivered to the dealer. Dealers seldom have all the cash available to make these advance payments for the cars they retail, so they are the first in line to arrange credit with a sales finance company or a bank. Lending agencies are glad to accommodate creditworthy dealers because, by financing their wholesale inventories, the lenders receive referrals of lucrative purchase contracts of the dealer's customers.

The automobile contract differs from a personal loan in that the proceeds of the loan are used to pay for the car. The finance company actually purchases each sales installment contract created when the dealer sells a car to an individual. The dealer makes all the arrangements at time of sale. Often he will write up the time-purchase contract on a form supplied by the finance company, which will then investigate the credit of the applicant prior to loan approval. The customer does not really own his car until all payments are completed, because the lender has the right to repossess the car (under specific conditions) in event of default anywhere along the line.

Once the customer signs the contract, he makes his payments directly to the lender, and has no recourse to the dealer who sold the car. There exists, however, an abiding relationship between the dealer and the finance company. This relationship is cemented by the finance company's agreement to pay an allowance, or commission, to the dealer on each installment contract. Almost invariably revenues generated from finance referrals represent a significant portion of automobile dealers' business profits.

The granting of retail credit for car purchases is big business. At the end of 1975 all short-term and intermediate-term installment credit outstanding in America totaled nearly $162 billion. Of that amount $53.6 billion was automobile credit. The largest sales finance companies are those owned by the Big Three motor companies: General Motors Acceptance Corporation, Ford Motor Credit Company, and Chrysler Financial Corporation. Other organizations prominent in this lending category are Commercial Credit Company, C.I.T. Financial Corporation, American Investment Company, General Acceptance Corporation, and credit unions. Commercial banks across the country are also very important in this business.

Installment contracts

To illustrate how a retail installment contract is set up, here is a transcript of an actual transaction, in this case on a small Chevrolet station wagon:

I.	Cash price of car (including power steering, radio, air conditioning, undercoat, and sales tax)	$4,217.90
II.	File fee	2.00
III.	Financing	602.84
	Total	$4,822.74
	Settlement	
I.	Cash deposit	300.00
II.	Used car traded in	825.90
III.	Payments: 36 @ $102.69	3,696.84
	Total	$4,822.74

Rising Auto Debts
Assumed by Finance Companies

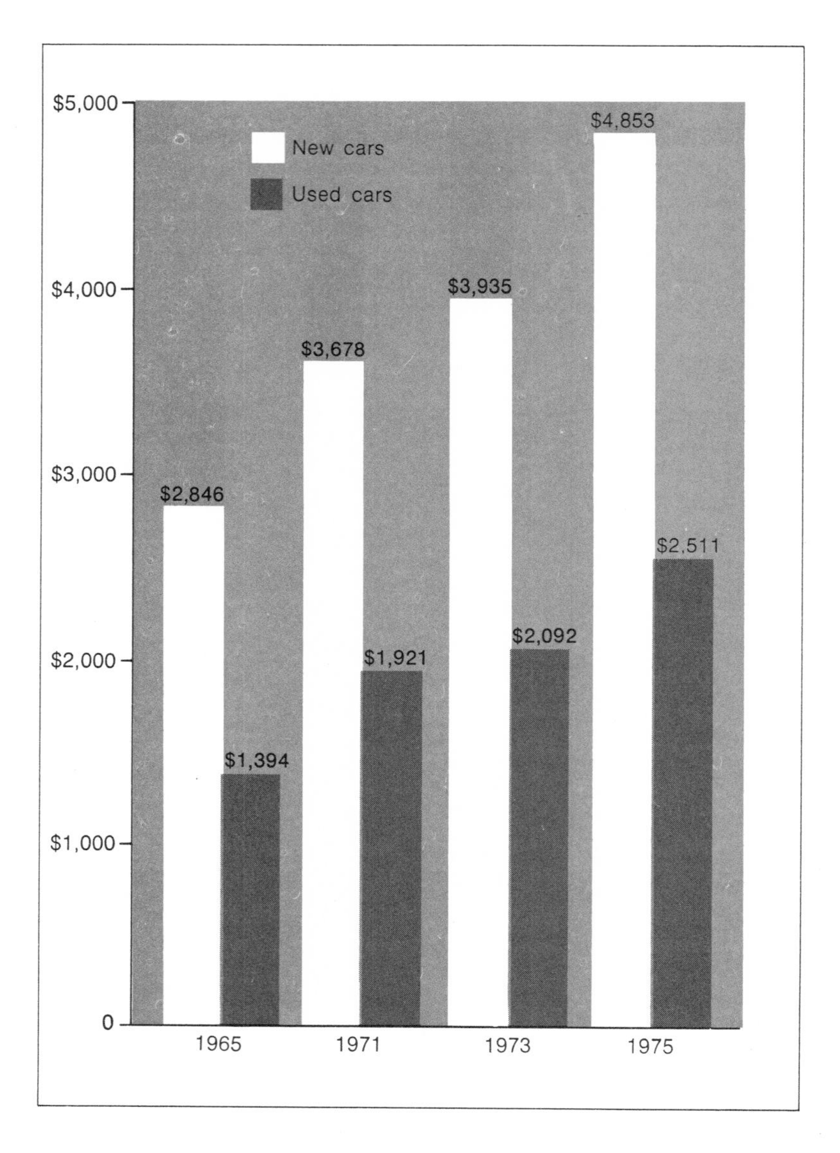

Note: Figures are averages.

Sources: Federal Reserve Board, National Consumer Finance Association

Although the time payments do not appear burdensome, the buyer pays $602.84 for the privilege of deferring outright ownership for thirty-six months; and the effective annual percentage rate of what amounts to a loan of $602.84 works out to 11.96 percent. This example is some months old, but a comparable transaction today would cost about the same because the car price would be higher and the effective interest rate would be less.

The contract just illustrated clearly states all the costs involved. Contracts written a few years ago were less explicit; and in some instances unscrupulous car credit companies concealed the true cost of the financing by lumping the sales price and financing together, deducting the trade-in or cash payment, and handing the customer a book of thirty-six payment coupons at so much a month.

Automobile finance charges are spelled out in the laws of many states. For example, in New York State, car finance companies may charge 7 percent for new cars, 10 percent for used cars up to two years, and 13 percent for older models. These interest rates are added on to the total amount of the unpaid balance at the time the car is delivered. Because you start paying off debt with your first payment and have prepaid interest on the total amount for the full payment period in advance, the true annual interest rate on the average amount you owe will be much higher than the state legal rates referred to above.

Loans from banks

Banks work along different lines and in effect lend you the money so that you may pay the dealer in cash and in full for the car. The bank looks to you, as the maker of the note, to pay off the loan, and regards the car as collateral until the note is retired. Banks sometimes discount the interest, and other times add it on to the face value of the loan; and will sometimes allow up to forty-eight months for payment, thus remaining competitive with finance companies. They generally request that from one-fifth to one-third of the cost of the new car be paid as down payment. A typical car loan from a bank takes this form:

Delivered price of car (with all the extras)	$5,300
Down payment made	– 1,628
Amount borrowed and paid by bank to dealer	$3,672

Then the buyer is left with a thirty-six-month note to the bank totaling $4,320, which includes a finance charge of $648. This note is systematically reduced by payments of $120 a month over a three-year period. The effective true interest on this contract is 10.88 percent, a bit lower than on the contract cited earlier.

In general, car loans from banks have been available at true interest rates slightly lower than those of finance companies, but banks usually insist on larger down payments so that their loans may be better secured. Persons shopping for the most reasonable rates should definitely consider bank financing, and also credit union financing, if it is available to them.

However, many buyers have their decisions virtually made for them if the car dealer acts as a representative of the finance company operated by the car manufacturer. It is so easy just to sit at a desk in the dealer's showroom and make all the financial arrangements, including the approval of your credit.

Further, certain sales finance companies may accept a marginal credit risk that a bank might reject, or might take a smaller down payment. Either way retail auto credit is a profitable business, and some prestigious companies have emerged as a result of concentrating their efforts in this field over the years.

Leader in field

The largest and best-known sales finance company is General Motors Acceptance Corporation (GMAC). It is a wholly owned subsidiary of General Motors Corporation. Its general business is to finance the acquisition by dealers for resale of new products manufactured by General Motors, and to acquire from such dealers retail installment obligations covering sales (including certain leasing transactions) of new products, as well as used units of any make. GMAC does not make direct loans, nor does it enter the transaction for purchase and financing of a car until the terms of sale are agreed upon by the dealer and his customer and the contract between these parties has been executed.

GMAC makes available, on an optional basis, debtor life insurance through a group policy written by the Prudential Insurance Company of America. In 1975, 15.9 percent of GMAC contracts were covered by Prudential term life insurance on the debtors.

Dealer arrangements with GMAC are not exclusive, and GMAC purchases only about 34 percent of General Motors dealers' new car time-payment sales. The remaining 66 percent is financed by banks, other sales finance companies, credit unions, and the dealers.

GMAC's installment credit business has risen steadily with retail volume increasing from over $6.4 billion in 1969 to $10.7 billion in 1977, plus $3 billion in lease financing. The number of new cars financed by retail installment and lease financing by GMAC in the United States in 1977 was 1,163,000. Outside the country, 224,000 units were financed.

Delinquency has not been a serious problem because

in a representative month 84 percent paid in response to past-due notices; and 8 percent paid after further prodding. One percent had their accounts extended or renewed; only about 2.5 percent were thirty or more days in default; and less than .5 percent had their cars repossessed for defaulting on payments.

In 1977 the average amount of GMAC contracts on new passenger cars and trucks in the United States was $6,205; on late models (within the last four model years), the average was $3,362. Comparable figures for 1969 were $3,533 and $2,065. The average length of contract on GMAC-financed cars in 1977 was 37.7 months, and the average payment was $163. These GMAC statistics appear to be fairly representative of the credit procedures and experience of other automotive finance agencies.

Chrysler Financial Corporation reported that it financed 408,655 new and used vehicles in this country during 1977. The average outstanding new vehicle balance was $6,287, and the average contract maturity was 41.6 months. In 1977 Chrysler financed 10.4 percent of the total new vehicle sales by Chrysler dealers, either by means of contract or lease by the Chrysler Credit Corporation.

Car credit is such a large business that competition tends to regulate lending practices, rates, and loan durations. The variations are found mainly in the used-car business, where unscrupulous dealers may trap the unwary with subtle overcharges.

It is obvious that car credit financing is a way of life, and an indispensable ingredient in the progress and profitability of the motor industry. For millions of Americans a car contract has a virtually permanent place in the family budget. When the three years of a car loan contract have expired, the old model, which has served as collateral for the loan, is traded in for a new model (and a new installment contract) ; and the cycle begins all over again. Based on estimates by the Federal Reserve Board and the U.S. Department of Commerce, payments on all automotive indebtedness represented 4.6 percent of disposable personal income in 1975, a figure virtually unchanged in recent years. Payment obligations seem to increase in ratio with incomes.

Compare rates

It definitely pays to shop for the best rates; but most people seem so eager to get their hands on a new car that they accept the first installment contract proposal offered and only ask how much the monthly payments will be. In the used-car business the sale is generally swiftly concluded if the amount of the monthly payment is attractive.

Used-car contracts generally run for about eighteen months because the sales price is much lower than for a new car. True interest rates on used-car credit are generally higher for several reasons: a used car is not as good collateral as a new car; used-car buyers are typically not as credit-worthy as those who can afford the latest model; and repossession is more frequent.

In all, about 275,000 cars are repossessed each year by all financing agencies on delinquent credit contracts. This amount may be on the increase due to the impact of the inflated cost of living on family budgets.

In arranging for a time-payment contract, first find out the actual cash delivered price, then deduct the trade-in or down payment you are making. The balance is what you will owe. Then ask for the total finance charge on that balance for, say, a thirty-six-month contract. The actual amount of this charge is what you should consider carefully. Compare it with the finance "package" offered by a second lender—a bank or another finance company. That way you will be sure that you are get-

When You Buy a Car

If you want to obtain the most credit at the least cost, shop for the lowest annual percentage rate (APR) when financing the purchase of an automobile. The figures given below are estimates of national averages.

To Finance $2,000 for 2 Years—

Lender	*APR*	*Credit Might Cost*
Life Insurance Policy	4-6%	$127
Credit Union	6-12%	260
Bank	8-15%	327
Savings & Loan Association	6-15%	327
Car Dealer	12-25%	574
Finance Company	12-30%	684

Source: Federal Trade Commission

ting the best deal, and you may be able to save a considerable amount in interest.

Prudence in timing your car purchase can help reduce financing charges. Used-car prices, which determine how much you get for the car you trade in, are usually higher in the spring, lower in the summer, and lowest between November and February. New cars depreciate about 30 percent in the first year and at the end of two years are worth about 50 to 55 percent of their price when new. Some people do very well by shopping for bargains among the previous year's models which dealers may be eager to sell to make way for their inventory of new models introduced each autumn.

To do well with automobile credit, do some comparative shopping, and do not sign up for payments so large that they will create budgetary problems. One way to avoid heavy monthly payments is to make a larger down payment if you can spare the cash.

In 1977 new cars cost approximately 8 percent more than in the previous year; forty-eight-month contracts were increasingly popular; and the average monthly payment was about $165. The cheapest way to buy a car these days (other than cash) is through a high down payment and a short-term installment contract.

Effect of inflation

The inflation in our economy which crested in 1974 could change the automobile credit picture considerably. If car prices increased due to higher costs of materials, labor, and transportation, and 13 to 15 percent interest rates prevailed, monthly installment charges might become too steep for buyers' incomes. They might buy fewer cars, or possibly default in far greater numbers, glutting the market with repossessed cars. If this should occur, the favorable credit experience and high profits enjoyed by lending agencies over the past forty years would end. However, if inflation should get completely out of control, contracts to pay off notes would be easier to manage because later payments would be made with greatly depreciated dollars, while the value of the cars, in terms of shrinking dollars, would actually rise.

FOR SALE

CHAPTER 10

Borrowing to Buy a House

A unique feature of American life is that about 65 percent of all families own their homes. Since 1970, however, this percentage has tended to decline because of the higher prices for housing.

The prices of single family houses across the country have steadily risen since the end of World War II. The cost of a comfortable single-family structure on a standard plot, in Levittown, Long Island, a major housing development, was about $16,000 in 1945. Today it would be $48,000 or more.

Interest rates in mid-1974 were the highest in a century. Mortgage interest in 1945 was 6 percent for a conventional mortgage, 4½ percent for a Federal Housing Administration (FHA) loan, and 4 percent for a Veterans Administration (VA) loan. Virtually all private home financing falls into one of these three categories.

The conventional mortgage is one that is not guaranteed or issued under regulations of a government agency. It is made between a lender and a borrower with its security provided by the solvency, integrity, and income of the borrower, and the market value of the real property under lien.

The largest originators of conventional mortgage loans are savings and loan associations, mutual savings banks, life insurance companies, commercial banks, and, in recent years, pension funds.

Conventional mortgages are made under the laws of each state, differing mainly in the maximum percentage of appraised value, or actual sale price, which may be used as the basis for issuance of a mortgage, and the legal maximum rate of true interest which may be charged under the usury laws of a given state. Six percent was fairly standard across the country for years, but because of inflation since 1970, most states have revised the top legal limit for interest rates. In 1977 it was 8½ percent in New York, 9 percent in New Jersey, and 9½ percent in California.

For a conventional mortgage under New York law, a savings bank or other institutional lender has, in the past, generally insisted on a down payment in cash of at least 20 percent of the purchase price of the property, and the balance secured by a first mortgage to be amortized in equal monthly installments over a period of thirty years.

Until 1932 most conventional home mortgages were not amortized but came due in full at the end of three to five years. The top rate for mortgages in those days was 6 percent; and many especially well secured or low percentage mortgages were arranged at 5½ percent. When the mortgage came due, it might be reduced by a modest

Increased Price of New One-Family Homes

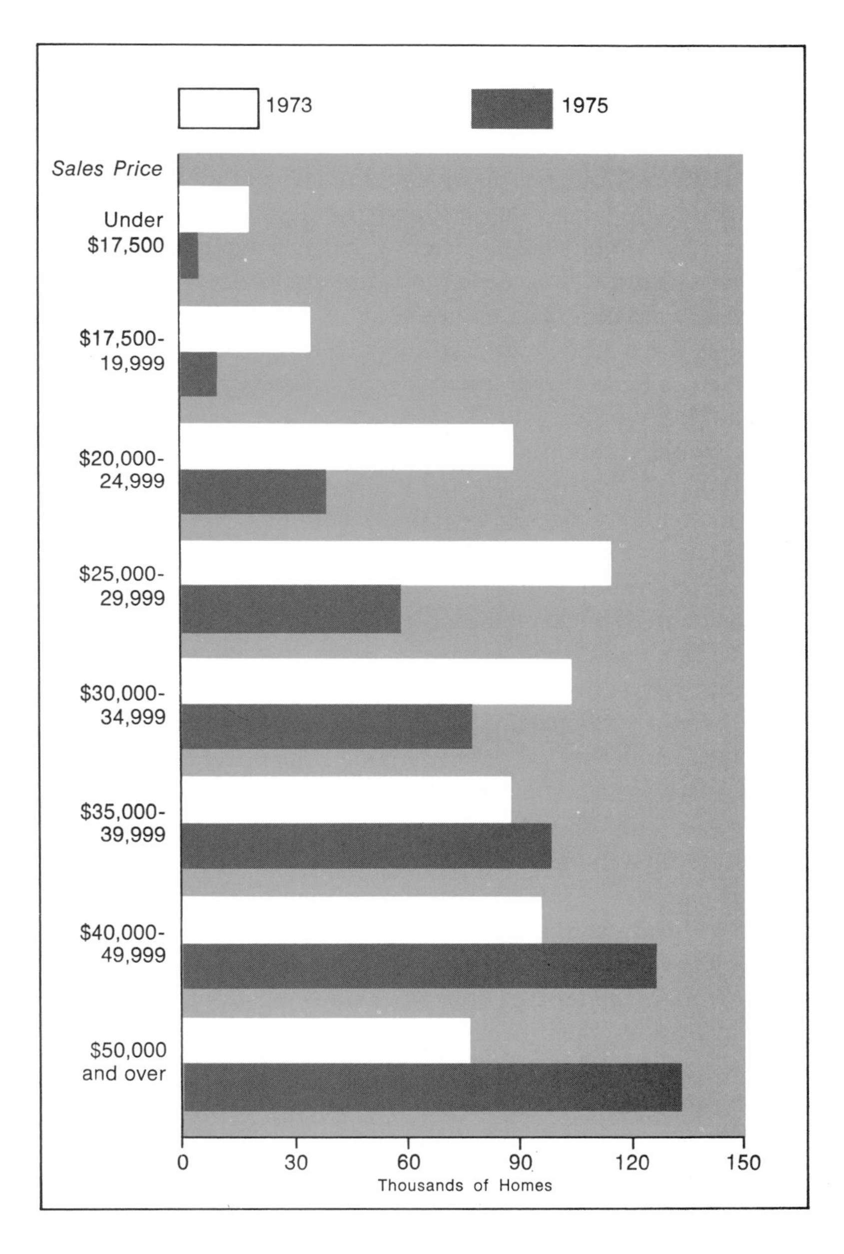

Source: Bureau of the Census

amount and then renewed for another five-year period.

The Great Depression changed all that because tens of thousands of mortgages came due in a period (1932-33) when mortgagors did not have funds with which to pay them off. Indeed, many could not even pay current interest and taxes. So the lenders foreclosed, and an army of anguished Americans lost their homes. These personal tragedies served to provide a new view of mortgages: that there was no need to have home mortgages come due in a lump sum in so short a period as five years; and that a longer repayment period, coupled with a provision for regular monthly reduction of principal, not only would create a reliable long-term source of income for the lender, but would steadily improve the quality of his loan and virtually eliminate delinquencies. Moreover, the owner would constantly build up the equity in his property and display a visible pride in its ownership.

Gradually the loan period was stretched, first from five to ten years, then to twenty years, and now twenty-five to thirty years is standard. This progressive extension of mortgage maturity is similar to the extension of the repayment period in automobile time purchases, but it is based on far more logical grounds, because houses have increased in value each year, while motor cars depreciate heavily from the moment they leave the showroom.

In 1977 the conventional thirty-year mortgage under New York state law carried an 8½ percent interest rate, and lenders generally requested, and received, a one-third down payment in cash.

FHA mortgages

The Federal Housing Administration loan was designed differently. It was intended to stimulate and facilitate home ownership by permitting the buyer to put less money down, and to have the mortgage issued at a higher percentage of valuation, and therefore was theoretically less well secured. Such a mortgage was guaranteed by the FHA, an agency of the United States government.

At the outset, the interest rate paid by the FHA mortgagor was lower than that for a conventional mortgage. However, in order to finance the guaranty, the buyer was required to pay ½ percent annually to the FHA Insurance Company. Thus, while a conventional mortgage might have called for 6 percent in 1945, an FHA mortgage cost 5 percent, or a 4½ percent regular rate, plus ½ percent to "insure the guaranty."

In 1974, however, money market changes placed FHA mortgages almost out of consideration, because the interest charged rose to 9½ percent, plus ½ percent insurance, making a total of 10 percent; and the guaranteed lending limit was set at $33,000. This provision made it necessary for the prospective buyer to pay in cash the difference between $33,000 and the purchase price of the house. The 8½ percent rate on a conventional mortgage made it more attractive than an FHA loan at 10 percent. However, applications for FHA loans increased after the mortgage limit was raised to $45,000 and the required down payment was reduced in 1974. By March 1978 the interest rate was down to 8¾ percent.

VA mortgages

The Veterans Administration loan was created to enable those whose regular earning career had been interrupted by military service to buy their own homes without a down payment and at a favorable interest rate on a mortgage partially guaranteed by the VA without any extra charge. When prices of houses were low, the $12,500 maximum guaranteed by the VA on a mortgage was adequate; and hundreds of thousands of veterans bought homes, and have experienced the exciting increase in the value of their property in the years since.

In August, 1974, however, the interest rate on VA loans was 9½ percent, and the maximum amount guaranteed was still $12,500, although prices of houses had greatly increased. This made it difficult for the prospective buyer of a $60,000 house to find a lender who would be willing to provide a 100 percent loan with only $12,500 of the $60,000 guaranteed by the VA.

Mortgage market problems

The home mortgage market changed drastically in the 1970s, and it has become increasingly difficult for young married couples to own their own homes, even though mortgages are available. Let us consider a typical case:

An attractive suburban home can be bought for $55,000, and the couple can produce $20,000 in cash. This is a little over one-third of the price, and is satisfactory to the lending institution. A thirty-year mortgage for $35,000 is arranged at 8½ percent interest, and the couple is to pay $7.68 a month per $1,000 of mortgage, making a $268.80 monthly total. This amount they contract to transmit each month for the next thirty years—a series of payments exactly calculated to pay off the $35,000 in full by regular reduction of principal, and also the 8½ percent interest payments on the declining unpaid balances. To pay $3,225.60 a year, the couple should have an annual income of more than $20,000.

At the closing there are additional expenses, generally about 2 percent of the mortgage, or $1,000, including lawyer's fee, title insurance, tax adjustments, state tax stamps, and appraisal fee. Continuing expenses, in addition to mortgage payments, will include insurance, taxes, and maintenance. A householder's policy, which includes fire, casualty, and liability, will cost approximately $450 a year for the $55,000 home; and taxes may average about 2½ percent of the purchase price. Maintenance costs should total about $350 a year, and heating (in a northern location) about $800 to $1,000 annually.

A typical mortgage such as we have described could not be arranged in early 1974 on a $55,000 home, under either VA or FHA terms, because of statutory loan limits. If, however, one of these guaranteed mortgages had been secured (on a lower-priced home), the monthly amortization cost at 9½ percent for a VA loan would have been $8.41 per $1,000; and for FHA (9½ percent plus ½ percent) 10 percent, or $8.78 per $1,000 per month.

The table on page 142, and other monthly schedules of charges presented, relate only to interest and amortization. Most lending institutions take it upon themselves to pay, or supervise payment of, taxes and insurance on mortgaged property; and they may require that a specified amount be added to the monthly payment to ensure that these related charges are regularly met.

Advantages and penalties

From the standpoint of the borrower, the mortgage is a useful vehicle enabling him to own a home otherwise beyond his reach, and a disciplining financial obligation that he must discharge with maximum fidelity. It is very much to the advantage of the mortgagor to fulfill his commitments and thus systematically increase the equity in his home.

If he defaults, he will incur serious penalties. In most states the mortgagor must meet his payments or lose his house. In event of default, he agrees to transfer deed, or convey title, to the lender and to undergo a foreclosure action that legally implements such transfer of title.

In certain states, California in particular, the mortgage itself vests the realty title with the lender, and the buyer secures it only after he has fulfilled all the provisions of the mortgage agreement. The mortgagor, in this

Home Loan Payment Calculator

To use the table, multiply the monthly payment-per-thousand shown by the number of thousands of dollars to be borrowed. The result will be the monthly principal-and-interest payment during the life of the mortgage.

Interest Rate	LENGTH OF MORTGAGE 20 Years	25 Years	30 Years
	Monthly Principal-and-Interest Payment per $1,000 of Mortgage		
7½ %	$8.06	$7.39	$7.00
7¾ %	8.21	7.56	7.17
8%	8.37	7.72	7.34
8¼ %	8.52	7.89	7.51
8½ %	8.68	8.06	7.68
8¾ %	8.84	8.23	7.87
9%	9.00	8.40	8.05
9¼ %	9.16	8.57	8.23
9½ %	9.33	8.74	8.41

Source: National Savings and Loan League

case, has possession; but the mortgagee is the legal owner, under what is called a trust deed. This arrangement makes unnecessary the delays and costs of a foreclosure action.

Generally, however, mortgage contracts describe the mortgagor as the actual owner of the property, and require him to warrant that it is free from all other encumbrance, claim, or lien, and to agree to defend and protect his title against any possible claim of ownership of, or interest in, the property by any other person or party. Because of this warranty, it is customary for the borrower to take out, and pay for, a policy of title insurance at the time of closing.

The other things the owner agrees to do are to pay all taxes, levies, and/or assessments on the property promptly (these may include real estate, water, sewer, or school taxes); to carry, and pay for, adequate fire and casualty insurance at all times; and to maintain the building and grounds satisfactorily. This latter obligation is usually enforced by a socially conscious community. Neighbors in a well-maintained residential area will put pressure on any householder who neglects the appearance of his property and thereby reduces the attractiveness of the neighborhood.

Recording the mortgage

It is vital that a mortgage, once created, be officially recorded. Mortgages are customarily recorded locally at a county clerk's office, often dignified by the title "Registrar of Deeds." The date and hour when the mortgage is actually recorded are important, because recording gives priority to the mortgage over any other lien that might be filed, and is official notice that the real estate has a lien against it. Equally, when the mortgage has been paid off, it is important that the county recorder be informed and that he issue an appropriate notice of release of lien to the borrower.

Mortgage lending is a massive industry carried on by a group of financial institutions. In order of their importance these lenders are: savings and loan associations, with total home loans of $225,332,000,000 at the end of 1975; life insurance companies, with $89,160,000,000; commercial banks, with $76,616,000,000; and savings banks, with $45,968,000,000. In addition, home mortgages in some volume are originated by pension funds, and by individuals who make personal mortgage loans (more frequently, second mortgages), usually in their own community and on properties that they can inspect personally at regular intervals.

Savings and loan associations

There are two kinds of savings and loan associations: the state and the federal. The state variety is generally smaller, and the borrower is offered a loan which he reduces through purchase of shares in the association in monthly installments, with interest charged on the unpaid balance until the mortgage is paid off. Federal savings and loan associations usually have larger capital funds; and the mortgages they hold are reduced and retired directly by monthly installments with interest charged on a steadily declining balance.

Historically, savings and loan associations have had the reputation of lending more liberally than savings banks; but that history had little reference to the 1974 lending market. Mortgage money became so tight in 1974 that all lending agencies could be very selective in the loans they arranged. Savings and loan associations did 44 percent of the national lending on one-to-four-family houses in 1965, and over 52 percent in 1977.

Life insurance companies

Life insurance companies have been traditionally conservative in lending on private homes. They generally have required a one-third down payment. However, because of their emphasis on top-quality liens, they have tended to charge somewhat lower interest rates. Some flexibility in their lending policy occurs when a new life insurance policy is bought from the company, to cover the declining principal amount of the mortgage, at the time the mortgage is arranged.

Savings banks

Mutual savings banks exist in seventeen states, and they have traditionally invested a very high percentage of their assets in home mortgages. The limits and conditions of lending are determined by the laws of the states wherein the banks are domiciled. As early as 1963 savings banks in New York were permitted to offer loans of up to 90 percent with up to thirty years for repayment. Interest rates charged have depended on the percentage of valuation, the age and quality of the structure, and the character and level of solvency of the borrower.

Commercial banks

Before World War II commercial banks confined most of their lending to personal, business, and commercial loans. As they increasingly sought and attracted time and savings deposits, they expanded rapidly into the field of home mortgages, often dealing with the same people who had had checking accounts with them for years. Home mortgages were another facet in the drive to offer "one-stop" banking.

Commercial banks have lent conservatively, generally preferring shorter maturities; and they have not insisted rigidly on monthly payments at a level to completely amortize the loan by maturity. Banks have been willing to accept regular reductions in principal for several years, and then renew an unpaid balance for several additional years.

Individual mortgagees

In the 1920s, ownership of home mortgages as an investment for well-to-do individuals was fashionable. That practice has fallen from general use, because institutions are better able to provide needed funds for longer periods, and have efficient organizations to supervise and service large loan portfolios. The constant attention of the investor to the condition of the mortgaged property and the need to see that taxes, insurance, and interest were promptly paid by the mortgagor made this type of investment less popular. Besides, individual mortgages have poor marketability, and, for use as collateral if needed, are less acceptable than stocks and bonds.

The main investment in home mortgages by individuals currently takes the form of second mortgages.

Home Mortgage Holders

(1950 vs. 1975)

1950

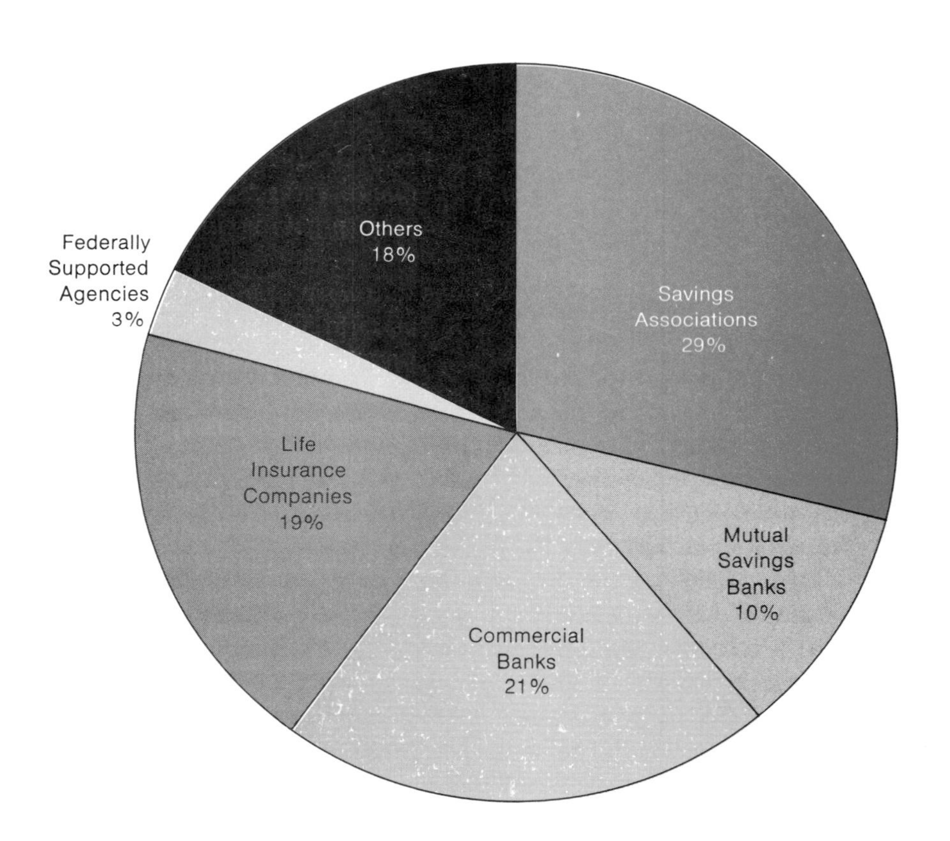

Note: Figures are for one- to four-family nonfarm homes.

Sources: Federal Home Loan Bank Board, Federal Reserve Board, United States League of Savings Associations

Home Mortgage Holders

1975

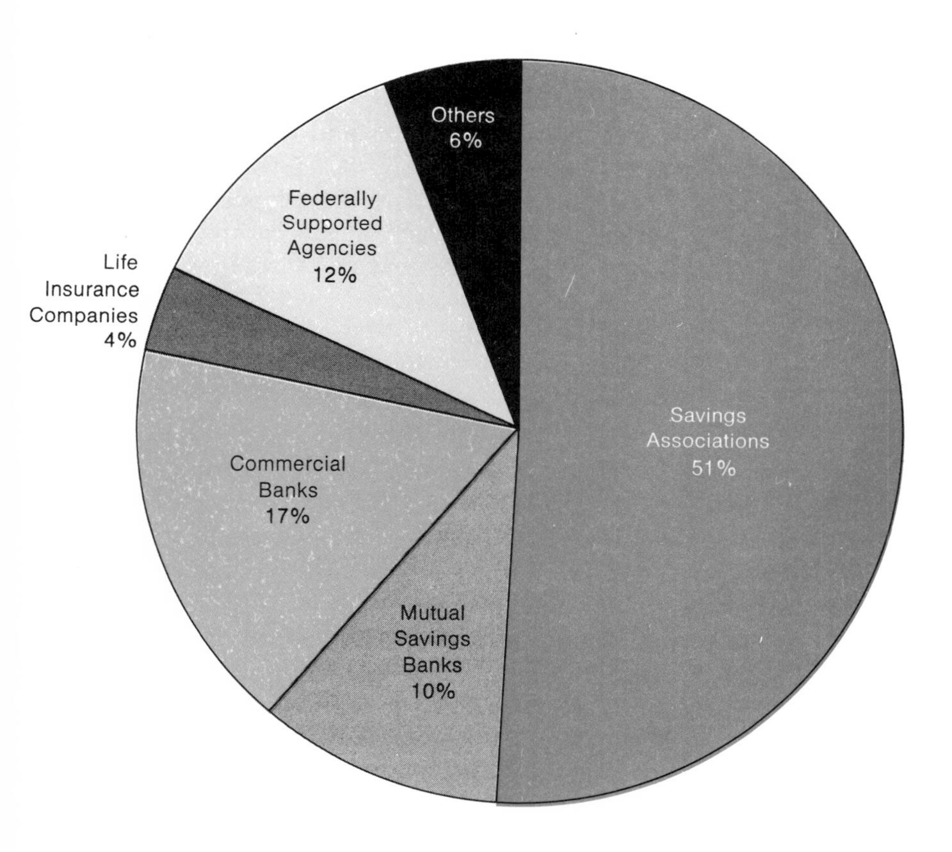

These can carry, depending on state laws, very high interest rates—12 percent and even more—and cover those cases where the home buyer does not have enough ready cash to meet the required down payment. In order to obtain a second mortgage often a buyer must give "points" as a bonus; a point is 1 percent of the loan.

A second mortgage may also originate when a house with an existing first mortgage is sold, and the seller accepts a second mortgage in lieu of a higher down payment by the buyer. Builders of housing developments who are anxious to sell their newly constructed properties may arrange "purchase money" second mortgages, enabling the buyer to acquire title with a very small down payment in cash.

Homeownership progress slows

For the average American family, the largest and most important investment ever made is in a home. Homeownership is a badge of security and independence, and a central influence in family life. Also, richly furnished homes on attractively landscaped grounds have always been major status symbols.

However, the progress of homeownership has been seriously slowed down in the 1970s for the reasons cited earlier: soaring home prices with correspondingly bigger mortgages. The yields on conventional home mortgages rose from 6.97 percent in 1968 to 8.78 percent in mid-1974, but have declined since. In addition, the traditional mortgage-lending institutions, particularly savings and loan associations and savings banks, have been hit by an economic phenomenon called "disintermediation." This means that people have drawn out money from their savings accounts in order to invest for higher returns in the bond market. The result has been that thrift institutions have had a lower volume of funds available for mortgage lending.

New trends in home mortgages

Important in any consideration of mortgages is the steady rise in price of both old and new houses in the United States. Individual home owners have realized remarkable windfall profits. For example, a house purchased in 1965 for $25,000 had increased in worth to $55,000 by 1978, a gain in equity of $30,000. Also the mortgage burden and amortization payments of older mortgages are light by current standards. In the past fifteen years the gain in market value of American single-family owner-occupied homes has been estimated at some $150 billion—a gain that continued even after 820,000 new single-family homes were built in 1977.

Home owners have capitalized on these gains in several ways. Some have sold their old houses and bought more expensive homes with new and larger mortgages. Other owners have renegotiated their mortgages, increasing them and releasing a portion of their equity gains for other purposes such as house additions or improvements, new cars, power boats, summer homes, cruises, or investments in stocks, bonds or rarities. Some experts have estimated that between $35 and $50 billion of these home-oriented capital gains were realized in 1977.

This trend probably will not continue at the 1977 rate for several reasons: (1) interest charges at 8¾ to 9 percent on new mortgages represent too high a monthly drain, especially on larger mortgages; (2) many home owners are reluctant to give up an older mortgage bearing a rate of 6 to 7 percent; and (3) some home owners, perhaps 10 to 15 percent, look forward to the day when they will own their homes "free and clear." The main goal of these owners is the reduction, not the increase, in mortgage obligations. This is particularly true of people nearing retirement age who stress maximum living income and seek to limit or eliminate their indebtedness.

Lenders also are mindful of the rise in home values and seek to lend to as many home owners as possible. Further, they have observed a shrinking flow of funds into savings institutions in recent years and would like to do something constructive about it.

One such development occurred in October 1977 when Congress passed the Housing and Community Development Act, which raised the limit on federally insured homes from $45,000 to $60,000. The loan ceiling for mobile homes was increased from $12,500 to $16,000. Also, the act provided for lower down payment requirements and boosted insurance limits on home improvements and mobile homes. Under new FHA provisions, a $40,000 home, conventionally mortgaged and requiring $8,000 down, can be secured with a down payment of as little as $1,500.

Mortgage insurance is big business. In 1977 the national placement mortgage loans on single-family homes totaled $150 billion. The Veterans Administration guaranteed mortgages on approximately 389,000 homes (78,000 new residences and 311,000 existing houses). FHA loans were on about 323,000 homes (50,000 new and 273,000 existing).

New mortgage ideas

In February 1978, the Federal Home Loan Bank Board, which serves 4,065 federally insured savings and loan associations and 74 mutual savings banks, published a ponderous three-volume study featuring the new mortgages it favors. These are the two main types:

The first is the graduated payment mortgage (GPM) with reduced monthly payments at the outset. For example, a conventional mortgage loan of 9 percent today requires payments of $241.39 per month. The new GPM would call for payments beginning at $196 per month and increasing by $15.90 per month each year until the sixth. Then the amount will have risen to $262 a month and will remain there for the life of the mortgage. The idea is to reduce the payment burden at the outset and increase it in line with presumed gains in the annual income of the home owner. It is obvious that this lower initial payment burden will enable thousands to buy homes, but it may also encourage people to buy larger homes than they can afford. With prices going up across the board, the home owner may find it difficult to meet the higher monthly payments due in the sixth year.

The second innovation is described by FHLBB as a "reverse mortgage." Under this plan, a home owner in the senior age bracket may borrow all or part of the equity in his home and apply the money to increase his income by purchasing a life annuity from an insurance company. Loan interest is regularly deducted and sent to the issuing savings and loan. At death, the house would be sold and the proceeds used to pay off the mortgage. The payments on the money borrowed to buy the annuity would be made over a seven-year period. If the owner cannot meet the payments and is forced to sell the house to meet them and to pay off the total mortgage, he may be in a bind—without a home and with diminished income.

These innovations, and mortgages with flexible interest payments that vary with the prime interest rate, are likely to gain considerable acceptance in the future; thus home owners should be familiar with them.

CHAPTER 11

Borrowing for Education

Although loans to finance education arrived rather late in the history of consumer credit, two factors have made educational lending increasingly important and, indeed, essential in the United States: the expanding percentage of our population which each year seeks higher education and the steadily rising costs involved.

In 1964 the average cost of a resident year in college was $2,000. Now the figure is about $6,000, with the outlay at an Ivy League institution running about $1,000 higher. Thus a family with two college-bound children is faced with an ultimate investment of over $40,000. This figure often is exceeded as more and more college alumni go on to professional and other graduate schools. In any event, $40,000 is a rather large amount to work into a family budget when allocating a middle-class annual income of, say, $20,000. So, for well over half of the college-oriented families, some form of borrowing and stretching out of payments is essential.

The long-term return on an investment in college education is considerable. A college-educated person will earn, on the average, almost three times as much in a lifetime as one whose formal education ended with a high school diploma. As our technology, medicine, finance, business, and government all become more complicated, specialized, and sophisticated, there is an increasingly insistent demand for a broad range of postgraduate capabilities. And, of course, collegiate experience is widely acclaimed for the personal, social, and cultural advantages it imparts that cannot be measured in terms of dollars or income tax brackets.

College education has indeed become a strived-for status symbol; so much so that many parents toil and sacrifice in order to give their children this advantage in life. The opportunity to borrow funds as needed, and to spread out repayment over several years is therefore not only welcome but often indispensable.

Many sources and kinds of loans are available to meet this quite pressing financial need. The most obvious are those credit programs and scholarships offered by the educational institutions themselves. In planning higher education for their children, parents should investigate carefully all avenues for financial aid available at the colleges and universities under consideration. That research alone may lead to a solution of the financing problem.

Loans by colleges

Scholarships are grants of money which need not be repaid. There is a wide assortment—scholastic, athletic, or money available from endowments for students meeting certain specifications. These have been around a long time, but the lending of tuition money did not really get under way until the onset of the Great Depression, when millions of families could not consider college for their children without substantial financial help. Massachusetts Institute of Technology established a sizable loan fund in 1931, charging interest at the friendly rate of 1 percent. Harvard College was one of the early entrants in the field and the pioneer, in 1953, in lending to freshmen. A great many private colleges and universities have since followed suit with various forms of credit accommodation, depending on the resources at their disposal.

While there are several loan plans whereby parents incur the obligations and sign the notes that pay college costs, the loans by colleges from their own funds, or from endowments under their control or supervision, are made directly to the student, who is solely responsible for interest charges and ultimate repayment in full. Such repayment may not occur until several years after graduation.

College loans to students whose families lack the funds for college expenses were originally based on the honor system. The student could borrow a portion of the money required without signing a note. He was expected to repay as rapidly as possible after graduation, so that other deserving students might have the same opportunity he or she had enjoyed. Interest on the loan was not expected, but it was hoped that those able to do so would make a financial contribution in addition to their repayments, in gratitude for the use of the money that had made possible their education.

This honor system was not completely satisfactory. Many alumni dragged out their payments; some never did repay in full. Experience therefore indicated that the loan should be legally as well as morally binding; and that, especially in periods of inflation and high interest rates, interest at agreed rates must be charged and collected.

Collegiate student loans nowadays generally accrue interest at a modest rate while the student is at school, increase the interest rate after graduation, and call for repayments to begin within nine months to a year after graduation. Provisions generally limit borrowing to no more than 75 percent of the needed money. Some schools limit loans to one-half of yearly expenses, and urge the borrowing student to finance the other half through part-time and summer vacation employment.

Loans to freshmen are less common because the staying power of the student has not been established. If the first-year student becomes discouraged, disinterested, or cannot get passing grades, and drops out, he or she may ignore or reject requests for repayment. In any event credit-worthy students are expected to maintain at least passing grades, and the possession of a scholarship is no impediment to obtaining a loan as well.

In practice, coeds have been less favored for credit, on the theory that many will marry shortly after graduation and thus will lack incomes of their own for repayment, and would not wish to burden their marriage with a sheepskin debit. Moreover, until quite recently, families in a financial squeeze seemed to regard sending their sons to college as more urgent than sending daughters. Thus college-bound girls have tended to come from wealthier homes where outside financing is less needed.

The student loan program at Columbia University seems fairly representative. At that institution, student loans may be made from university funds or from certain controlled endowments. The maximum loan, except under special circumstances, is $4,000, and carries a 3 percent interest charge per annum on the unpaid balance. Repayment is expected to begin nine months after graduation and at a rate of at least $30 a month; and the entire amount is to be repaid, with interest, no later than ten years after graduation.

Colleges and universities, pressed by rising costs and some falling off in registrations, do not have sufficient funds available to meet in any significant way the needs of students who lack cash. Fortunately, several other sources of financial aid have come on the scene and are helping to solve the problem. Of these agencies, the most important is the United States government, through its guaranteed student loans.

Guaranteed loans

In the early 1960s the federal government, under the National Defense Education Act, began a loan program for freshmen and upperclassmen, arranged through colleges and universities. The program offered loans of up to $1,000 a year, repayable over ten years with interest at 3 percent. There was also a provision that if, after graduation, the student became a teacher in a public school, up to 50 percent of his loan might be forgiven at the rate of 10 percent for each year of teaching.

This lending by the government, now called National Direct Student Loans, continues, as does the Guaranteed Student Loan Program, providing for insured student loans, originated and serviced by banks and other credit agencies, states, and eligible educational institutions. This plan is based on loans to students. It is operated by the U.S. Office of Education and is aided by the Student Loan Marketing Association (popularly called Sallie Mae), a government-sponsored private corporation created (by 1972 amendments to the Higher Education Act of 1965) to provide liquidity, entirely through instituting secondary market and "warehousing" facilities for insured student loans made by eligible lenders under the Guaranteed Student Loan Program (GSLP).

To be eligible to participate in the association, a lender

usually must own at least 100 shares of Sallie Mae. Eligible lenders include institutions, state agencies, financial or credit institutions, and insurance companies, which are subject to examination and supervision by an agency of the United States or a state, and pension funds approved by the commissioner of education.

As of July 1, 1977, over eight million loans had been made under the GSLP for more than $8 billion.

Under Sallie Mae, student loans made by eligible lenders and institutions may be insured either by the United States government or by a nonfederal program (which may have loans reinsured, up to a certain percentage, by the government). The U.S. Office of Education has found that as of July 1, 1976, about $4.8 billion of insured loans were outstanding. Sallie Mae may purchase loans from originating lenders or make warehousing loan advances to them, backed by collateral equal to at least 125 percent of the principal amount of such advances, consisting of guaranteed student loans bearing interest of at least 7 percent.

The theory behind this somewhat complicated procedure, involving a guaranty and buying loans from institutions or lending to them on collateral, is to promote, implement, and facilitate higher education in the United States. It is recognized that, from a financial lender's viewpoint, student loans run for too long and cannot bear in full the interest rates that are customarily charged for commercial, personal, or installment loans. The student is charged only 7 percent interest, with lenders given an allowance of up to an additional 3 percent (to the extent that current money market conditions impede the carrying out of the government program), when lenders might otherwise be earning a less than equitable rate of return in any given quarter of the year.

The government may agree to indemnify the originating lender for loss of principal and, in some cases, allow a supplementary amount of up to 3 percent so that the lender is not penalized by receiving a lesser return than that provided by prevailing interest rates.

Here are the rules for government-insured loans:

1. The loan must be made to a student who is enrolled and in good standing, or has been accepted for enrollment, at an eligible educational institution, on at least a half-time basis.

2. The loan must be made by an eligible lender.

3. The loan limits are $2,500 in a calendar year, with the aggregate principal amount not to exceed $10,000 at any time for both undergraduate and professional study. (The average size of loans made since 1968 is over $900.)

4. The principal must be repaid in monthly installments within a period of ten years, beginning within twelve months after active student life ends, with the minimum repayment being $360 during each year of the period. Each loan must be repaid not later than fifteen years after origination, with some exceptions made for those who return to school or join the Peace Corps.

5. The interest to be paid by the borrower is not to exceed 7 percent.

If a borrower, under any GSLP loan made after December 15, 1968, dies or becomes permanently disabled, the government, by means of insurance coverage, defrays the entire balance of principal and interest owed.

A virtue of this program is its flexibility. Loans may be arranged anywhere in the nation, and not only the institutions of learning themselves, but states and banks can originate and service them. States appreciate the arrangements for selling, or borrowing on, loan portfolios instead of having to set aside very substantial funds from their own budgets to stake thousands of youngsters to higher education via the loan window.

Some banks may not be enthusiastic about these student loans, but the guaranty protects them; and loan volume may be desirable to them, particularly when commercial lending is trending downward.

The record for lending funds to college or university students has been deplorable. The default rate on government-financed loans (minimum repayment is $30 a month starting nine months after graduation) is about 30 percent, and many students have gone through bankruptcy after college, just to get rid of this debt.

In February 1978 Joseph A. Califano, Jr., Secretary of HEW, stated that over $400 million was owed to the government by 344,000 former students who had received federally guaranteed loans through private banks; $600 million is still owed by students receiving direct loans from a government loan fund.

Educational loans to parents, instead of to students, have been far more satisfactory to lenders. There is, indeed, a new drive in the Ivy League to provide loans to middle-class parents to help pay for their children's education. Most recent to adopt such a plan was Dartmouth, which has begun a loan program for students entering in the fall of 1978 (the class of 1982). Loans bearing 9 percent interest will be made available to families with incomes of up to $75,000 a year. Harvard, Yale, Amherst, Princeton, Smith, and Stanford now make similar loans available.

Other student loans

For those who go on to graduate schools, there are many student loan opportunities. Engineering schools may be able to make sizable advances—up to $10,000. The Ford Foundation has loan money available for graduates who wish to become teachers or university faculty members. These loans go as high as $10,000, with the debt canceled at the rate of $1,000 a year or 20 percent of the amount, whichever is greater, when the loan recipient becomes, and while he remains, a professional educator. If the borrower does not become a teacher, he or she must repay the loan on a gradual basis at 3 percent interest.

The American Medical Association Education and Research Foundation (AMA-ERF) has an extensive loan program for medical students who have completed their first semester or quarter, interns, and residents. It is the result of a cooperative effort by the medical profession and other sectors of the community.

Physicians have given generously to support this program, as have the Women's Auxiliary of the American Medical Association, private foundations, business, and industry. The pharmaceutical firm of Merck Sharp & Dohme was the first representative of private industry to provide major support of the guaranty fund. The Continental Illinois National Bank and Trust Company of Chicago was the first bank to make these loan funds available and is the principal participating bank. There are now many other participating banks across the country.

The need of each applicant is determined by the AMA-ERF Educational Committee and the bank that will make the loan if the application is approved. The loan, restricted to finance only normal expected expenses of a medical education, must be covered by a note signed by the applicant and cosigned by his wife if he is married. The maximum amount that can be borrowed in a twelve-month period (from September 1 to August 31) is $1,500, and the minimum note is for $400. The maturity date is the first day of the fifth month following the month of entry into the armed services or the completion of medical training including internship and any residency training, whichever is earlier. Interest rates are established quarterly on the basis of the prime rate in existence at the beginning of each calendar quarter: 1 percent over the prime rate during the training period, and

2 percent over the prime during the repayment period.

If the borrower defaults and fails to fulfill his obligation to the participating bank, the AMA-ERF buys the note from the bank, pays all interest due up to the time of default, and endeavors to collect the outstanding principal and interest directly from the student.

NARI loans

The National Association of Residents and Interns, in New York, also makes available a range of loans that are tailored to the needs of would-be doctors. For students in medical, dental, and osteopathic schools who have begun their senior year, $1,500 to $2,600 is available on a deferred principal payment basis, with only interest charges to be repaid during the first year of the loan. This type of loan is not available in California, Washington State, or Wisconsin. For NARI members who are residents, interns, or fellows, $5,000 is available in a lump sum. Repayment in conveniently low monthly installments begins forty-five days after the funds are received. Loans of $5,000 are also available to those members in military service, on the same basis.

When the medical student is entering, or already in, practice, up to $20,000 is available from NARI for purchase of medical or X-ray equipment, furniture, fixtures, office decorations, or general working capital. The advance of funds may begin within three months of termination of training. NARI members are also offered 100 percent financing for leasing or purchasing equipment, with up to seven years to repay the loan. If the physician wishes to purchase a car, he can obtain funds to cover its full cost—up to $5,000 to be financed—and extend repayments over five years. A member in good standing can also borrow $2,000, free of interest for ninety days through APPA/NARI Federal Credit Union. The charges on NARI credit extension run, depending on the specific use of the money and the duration of the loan, between 12.5 and 16.7 percent true interest.

The Tuition Plan

One of the oldest and a very widely used educational finance accommodation is The Tuition Plan, which was originated, sponsored, and introduced in 1938 by CIT Financial Corporation, a prominent sales finance, personal loan, and banking association.

This plan varies from the loans described earlier in that it involves the parent, not the student, in a direct consumer installment obligation, running for a maximum of seventy-two months. The arrangement is flexible and designed to include not only tuition costs but room, board, textbooks, and transportation; medical, music, and laboratory fees; and fraternity or sorority expenses.

This inclusive coverage—with life insurance on the parent available to assure completion of the child's education—has been used by more than half a million families. It supplies money for education at any school, college, or university, including study abroad; and has been accepted at over 2,600 schools and colleges as an alternative to paying educational costs in cash.

The Tuition Plan spreads the heavy expenses of education, which are concentrated, and often converge at an inconvenient time, over a period of years, thus flattening out peaks of monetary demand. For this reason it is desirable to start the program some months in advance of receiving the first tuition bill.

Bank loans

Commercial banks in many cities have developed their own direct personal loan plans for parents of the college-bound. For example, the Manufacturers Hanover Trust Company in New York offers what it calls Any

The Tuition Plan's Loan Programs

The tables show the interest costs, the size of monthly payments, and the cash amounts received. Annual percentage rates vary from 13.62 to 17.94 percent depending on the amount and term.

Two-Year Programs

Parent Receives		*Monthly Payments*		
Each Year	*2-Year Total*	*24 Payments*	*36 Payments*	*48 Payments*
$2,000	$ 4,000	$178.02 $4,272.48*	$127.80 $4,600.80*	$102.71 $4,930.08*
3,000	6,000	266.69 6,400.56*	191.15 6,881.40*	153.08 7,347.84*
4,000	8,000	355.12 8,522.88*	254.15 9,149.40*	202.79 9,733.92*
5,000	10,000	443.32 10,639.68*	316.78 11,404.08*	251.84 12,088.32*

Four-Year Programs

Parent Receives		*Monthly Payments*		
Each Year	*4-Year Total*	*48 Payments*	*72 Payments*	*96 Payments*
$2,000	$ 8,000	$178.02 $8,544.96*	$135.16 $9,731.52*	$115.14 $11,053.44*
3,000	12,000	266.34 12,784.32*	201.14 14,482.08*	170.55 16,372.80*
4,000	16,000	354.20 17,001.60*	266.05 19,155.60*	224.50 21,552.00*
5,000	20,000	441.60 21,196.80*	329.88 23,751.36*	277.01 26,592.96*

*Total of payments (monthly payment multiplied by number of payments).

School Loans, providing from $1,200 to $15,000 in funds to cover the costs of tuition, room, board, laboratory fees, textbooks, and clothing for just about any school, college, or university in the world.

The term of the loan is flexible, running from two to seven years, and it is calculated at a true interest rate of 11 percent. The bank arranges availability of the desired sums, which are advanced on an annual or semiannual basis, with the stipulation that there be at least three disbursements by the receiver of the loan over a period of eighteen months. The borrower may discontinue the arrangement at any time, with no obligation to accept the unused portion of the loan. Free life insurance on the borrower assures completion of the educational objective should the borrower die.

At Manufacturers Hanover Trust, a $10,000 loan with two $1,250 disbursements a year calls for a total loan of $11,431.36 for forty-eight months at $238.54 per month, including life insurance. Interest is at the rate of 11.4 percent. Variations of this type of credit are available at dozens of banking institutions in the country.

Loans that may be obtainable from churches, fraternal societies, clubs, and civic organizations round out the opportunities generally available to deserving students who are low on financial resources.

Parents and students should explore and compare all the available sources of credit in an endeavor to solve their problem at the lowest possible cost. The first place to check is the college itself or an organization sponsoring professional education; then check the possibilities of state funding or bank-insured loans under the GSLP, and direct, long-term consumer loans widely offered by banks and finance companies. The money is available; it is just a question of obtaining it on the most favorable terms.

WALL ST

CHAPTER 12

Borrowing to Buy Securities

Long before the credit card was even heard of, people had been borrowing money to buy securities. Indeed, the custom became a mania in the late 1920s just before the Great Depression. The purchase of securities, particularly common stocks, largely on borrowed money is serious business and should not be entered into lightly.

Do not even consider buying securities, much less buying them on margin, unless your financial house is in good order. Marketable investments should await the building up of surplus funds—money not needed for routine living expenses, systematic savings, and life insurance programs. Persons who are experiencing difficulty in meeting their financial needs are not ready to buy marketable securities, either outright or on credit.

Before entering the stock market, financial counselors

suggest that you have a savings account equal to one-third of your annual income. You need this liquid fund in case of emergencies. A serious accident or illness in your family can drastically increase your expenses; an economic slowdown may reduce your income or even put you out of a job. So make some provision for the unpredictable via a savings account.

The next prerequisite to investment is usually life insurance, in an amount perhaps equal to at least three years of your gross income. Try to strike a balance between lowest-cost term insurance, convertible to "ordinary life," and permanent cash-value insurance.

Investment portfolios

After attending to these preliminaries and considering the level of your income, your spending priorities, the price of housing, and possibly acquisition of your own home, you are ready to examine the structure of an investment portfolio. Traditionally this has meant starting out with government or high-grade corporate bonds and then working into some seasoned and quality-rated common stocks, which might include General Motors, American Telephone & Telegraph, Union Pacific, Pacific Gas and Electric, Sears Roebuck, Coca-Cola, Wrigley's, or American Home Products.

Marketable securities are just what their name implies: they are bought and sold each day on security exchanges or in the over-the-counter market; and they fluctuate continuously. Even the highest grade of common stock may vary by 25 percent or more in its market value in the course of a year. Stock values rise in times of good business and high confidence, and fall in times of confusion and uncertainty when earnings decline and dividends are reduced or eliminated.

The market newcomer, buying his first stock, generally expects it to advance in price, or at least not go down, and may experience great anxiety when stocks decline drastically as they did in 1929-32, in 1970, and again in 1974. So, regardless of your income, it is unwise to buy stocks either for cash or on credit if their fluctuation (particularly on the "down" side) is going to worry you. In such a case it would be better to keep your money in a savings account or to choose more stable investments such as AAA bonds.

Assuming that you feel able to bear the market's gyrations without undue strain, your purchases will probably be motivated by two main considerations: you want to invest in growing companies that can build a second income for you because they pay dependable dividends and may increase them as their profits expand; and you anticipate that, over a period of time, the stocks you acquire will become more valuable, thus increasing your net worth and offsetting inflation and the rising cost of living.

Buying on margin

You can always buy stocks for cash, transfer them into your name, and stow them away in a bank vault or other secure place. However, if you are confident about economic conditions generally, and favorably impressed by the results of researching specific issues by an informed brokerage or investment firm, an investment advisory service, or a responsible journal of finance, you may wish to buy more shares of an apparently promising stock than your cash resources will permit. Can you do this? Of course, by borrowing money from a bank or, more commonly, by buying on margin through a broker who lends you the money you need to increase your purchasing power. In taking either of these courses you are leveraging your transaction, i.e., using other people's money to increase the possible earning power of your own.

If, for example, you buy 100 shares of AT&T at 60, and pay cash, you will invest (not counting the brokerage fee) $6,000. If the issue advances to 70, you will have an indicated profit of $1,000 or a capital gain of 16.6 percent. Suppose, however, that to achieve a greater percentage return on your investment you buy the 100 shares on margin. To do this, under the 1978 regulations, you would have to put up 50 percent in cash, or $3,000, and borrow a similar amount (on which you will pay interest) from the broker. Then if the shares of AT&T bought at 60 go to 70, your indicated profit is still $1,000; but $1,000 represents a gain of 33.3 percent on your $3,000. Had you used the entire $6,000 required for the cash transaction, you would have bought 200 shares instead of 100 by margining; and that $6,000 would have earned a profit of $2,000.

It is this opportunity to make your money work harder for you that is the lure of buying on margin. It is delightful when stocks go up, but when they go down you lose twice as fast. To illustrate, if your AT&T shares, bought at 60, went down to 50, the $3,000 you invested would have been reduced by $1,000 to $2,000; and if the issue fell to 30 in a dreadfully distressed market, you would have been "wiped out"—unless you put up more margin. In any event, when your margin fell below $3,000, your broker would probably telephone you to ask for more money; and if you failed to produce it, he would "sell you out" at the then prevailing market price.

Margin rates

The requirements for a margin account are uniform among firms having membership on the New York Stock Exchange (NYSE). The actual percentage of margin (your money) required is determined by the Federal Reserve Board and is adjusted at intervals in response to the prevailing market climate. Historically, the percentage has ranged from 10 percent (before Federal Reserve regulation) to 100 percent. In 1973, the margin requirement was 65 percent. On January 3, 1974, it was reduced to 50 percent, and has not changed since.

In general, margin rates are increased as the market advances, to put a brake on overzealous speculation; and reduced when the market is descending or in a lower range.

Naturally, brokers prefer lower margins, so that their customers can purchase more stock by borrowing their money; and the more shares bought, the larger the broker's commissions.

It is generally believed that one of the reasons for the great market decline in 1929 was the low margin required (margin rates at that time were unregulated), usually 10 or 15 percent. A stock needed only to sell off from 100 to 85 to wipe out a speculator, unless he was able to raise additional funds. If he was able to put up another 10 percent and the stock descended further from 85 to 75, he was again wiped out. The distressed selling by thousands of anguished stock owners in 1929 exerted a domino-like effect in driving share prices steadily downward.

We do not need to go back to 1929 for examples of disaster in margin accounts. In June, 1974, Damon Corporation common stock, listed on the NYSE, closed at 25⅝ on a Thursday. In light of a company report of disappointing quarterly earnings, trading in the issue was halted the next day (Friday). The stock did not resume trading until the following Monday, when the issue opened at 12:45 P.M. at a price of 9½ on a 165,000-share block. Brokers did not have sufficient time to send out margin calls, and some margin buyers who received calls were not able to raise the needed funds. The brokers had a further problem in trying to collect from those who had taken such a rapid financial beating.

Rules for margin accounts

Requirements for a margin account are: a minimum of $2,000 cash, a 50 percent minimum margin on stocks purchased, and payment of interest on the borrowed balance. The annual interest rate on the daily net debit balance in the customer's account is computed at a selected rate above the prime money rates or on actual cost of borrowing the money, whichever is higher. The rules require a minimum of ½ percent over the prime rate, but the rate charged may be higher, depending on the size of the debit balance and the amount of commissions generated. Further, the interest rate applying to the margin account may be increased or decreased at any time without notice to the customer. Each purchase on margin adds to the debit balance, increases the amount of margin required, and raises interest charges.

Brokers have different levels at which they call for additional margin, but most would communicate with the customer by the time his equity drops to 30 percent. The minimum carrying equity under NYSE rules is 25 percent. In declining markets, keeping after customers for margin is an unpleasant and often recurrent task for brokerage firms.

Tens of thousands of investors discontinued their market activities entirely due to loss—both on margin and outright—in the decline of 1973-4. The total number of American shareholders is believed to have declined from 32.5 million in 1970 to 26 million at the beginning of 1977.

Not all stocks can be purchased on margin. Generally they must be listed on a major exchange and sell for more than $5 a share. Only a special list of over-the-counter stocks qualifies for margin purchase.

The securities you buy on margin become collateral

for your debt and are held by the broker in his name. Although the broker retains the certificates, you receive all the dividends, retain the right to direct the voting of your stock, and can sell it whenever you wish. The settlement dates for purchase or sale of stocks are exactly the same as for cash accounts—five business days following the transaction. When you open a margin account you must evidence satisfactory financial resources and responsibility and sign a margin agreement and a loan consent enabling the broker to pledge or lend securities carried in your account.

Margin buying is big business. In March 1977 total margin debt stood at $8.1 billion and this did not include securities held in loan accounts in commercial banks.

Bank borrowing

Commercial banks do a large lending business with securities as collateral. If you obtain credit to buy securities in this way, you will usually arrange the bank loan in advance. The bank will receive from your broker, and pay for, the stocks you have ordered, and debit your checking account, using a cash amount you agree to make available, plus the proceeds of the loan agreed on, for which you sign a note. The interest rate on the note will be about the same as you would pay on a debit balance at a brokerage firm. The end result is the same as with a margin account. You lack custody of the securities, and you pay interest on the borrowed balance. Dividends or interest received on the pledged securities are credited to your account and may substantially offset interest charges. You will, of course, be asked to supply additional cash if your securities decline significantly.

Under government regulations, banks are expected to observe the same margin requirements as brokerage firms whenever their customers seek to borrow money to buy stocks; but when dealing with a bank certain loopholes are available. The client may insist that his is a "nonpurpose" loan, or that he has some objective in borrowing other than buying securities. He may, in fact, borrow the required cash, or most of it, just on his signature at the bank, and then use those funds for an outright purchase at a brokerage firm.

There is a broad variety of securities acceptable as collateral. Most preferred are government and high-rated corporate bonds; probably second are top-quality preferred stocks; then blue chip common stocks listed on the NYSE; next, bank and insurance stocks traded for the most part over the counter; and, last, assorted utility and industrial securities traded in the over-the-counter market. (Hundreds of active over-the-counter issues now qualify for the same treatment as margin collateral as "listed" stocks.) Banks will also lend money on municipal bonds and mutual fund shares. Brokers and banks naturally prefer as collateral high-quality, actively traded securities. When loans are considered on securities of inferior investment quality or with inactive markets, they are usually calculated at lower percentages of valuation, and often bear higher interest rates.

Other lending agencies

Many people with meager resources, lured by the high percentage of capital gains they may realize in bull markets by operating heavily on borrowed money, explore ways to beat the margin requirements. One method employed is to purchase new issues of government bonds, available for individual subscription through banks, with the customer putting up only 5 or 10 percent of the purchase price. Government bonds are a prime form of collateral and the bank will assume that a new issue, attractively priced, will be unlikely to decline by as much as 5 percent. If an investor puts up $5,000 to purchase bonds with a par value of $100,000, and the issue advances one point (from 100 to 101), his profit, exclusive of interest on the loan (and offset by the interest he collects on the bonds), will be $1,000 or a 20 percent return on the $5,000 risked. Frequently profits of this type have been realized within a few days.

There are also agencies that will lend money on highly marketable securities with as little as 10 percent margin, although during a time of declining markets these sources become scarce. Wealthy individuals or special kinds of finance companies may lend on this thin margin but will charge interest at a rate of 18 percent or more. Suppose you buy 1,000 shares of General Motors at 50, investing only $5,000 of your own money. The interest on the loan will cost you $8,100, so you will need a healthy rise in GM in order to make any money; and if the stock sells off to 45, your $5,000 will be lost. Most people who speculate on a shoestring in this manner wind up in deep trouble, which may include getting in the clutches of a loan shark. There are very few securities, if any, so certain to advance as to warrant borrowing so heavily and so dangerously to buy them.

Exercising "rights"

There is another quite sophisticated way to borrow via the exercise of "rights" to buy a new "listed" issue. Assume that a seasoned company offers its share owners one new share at $40 for each ten shares held, at a time when the issue is selling on the stock exchange at $50. Many existing stockholders may decide not to subscribe and instead to sell their rights at an indicated price of about $1 apiece (ten rights are needed to subscribe to one new share). So you put up $10 for ten rights and $2.50 of your own money, and arrange through your broker to subscribe. If you buy 100 shares in this way your cost will be $12.50 per share, $1,250 in total, or 25 percent margin at the assumed stock exchange quotation of $50. If you had bought 100 shares of the stock at $50, without reference to the rights, you would have been required to provide 50 percent margin, $2,500, instead of $1,250 via the rights.

This type of specialized margin purchase has been available in the case of subscriptions to convertible preferred stocks or convertible bonds, "when issued." (Convertible bonds are generally acceptable as collateral at 40 percent instead of the current 50 percent required for stocks.)

Commodity trading

For those of a daring nature, there is also available the whole area of margin trading on commodities. Here you buy contracts to receive for future delivery, often months away, standard amounts of such staples as wheat, corn, soybeans, beef, copper, lead, and silver. You need put up only 10 percent margin. Commodities, however, behave in startling ways: a relatively small price swing in a $10,000 contract can deliver a swift profit or dismal loss and a call for more money.

While borrowing and risking capital on commodities is perfectly legitimate, it is a type of speculation that should be reserved for highly sophisticated and well-informed traders or outright gamblers. For the average person, commodity trading is too hazardous; and often the broker who solicits this business is not sufficiently informed on all the supply-demand factors, the weather prospects in the wheat belt, the possibilities of a strike or a revolution in a remote copper-producing country; or other current conditions that are sensitively and swiftly reflected by changes in commodity prices. Shrewd, informed, and lucky traders have made killings in commodities, but the odds are heavily against most investors doing so.

There is nothing wrong with borrowing money to enable you to buy a larger amount of desirable securities than your immediately available cash resources might permit. However, be on guard against borrowing too large an amount, paying too high an interest rate, and borrowing to buy at the wrong time, near market highs when a dip can swiftly erode or eradicate your equity.

Deal with a strong bank or well-resourced brokerage firm; make a plan to reduce your indebtedness over a specified period of time; and do not take a long business trip or vacation while you have an open margin account.

Borrowing to invest makes sense only if it offers reasonably safe prospects for increasing your net worth. Never buy a security without first getting the facts about it and a realistic evaluation of its profitable potential.

CHAPTER 13

Truth in Lending

The whole business of consumer credit has grown so rapidly, affected so many people, and led to such extensive abuses that the Congress, in due course, took note of the problem and passed, on May 29, 1968, Public Law 90-32, popularly known as the Truth in Lending Act. Its findings and declaration of purpose are summarized as follows:

> Sec. 102. The Congress finds that economic stabilization would be enhanced and the competition among the various financial institutions and other firms engaged in the extension of consumer credit would be strengthened by the informed use of credit. The informed use of credit results from an awareness of the cost

> thereof by consumers. It is the purpose of this title to assure a meaningful disclosure of credit terms so that the consumer will be able to compare more readily the various credit terms available to him and avoid the uninformed use of credit. (82 Stat. 146; 15 U.S.C. 1601.)

The act specifically excludes credit for business and commercial purposes, transactions in security or commodity accounts by broker-dealers registered with the Securities and Exchange Commission, credit transactions (except in real property) with total financing in excess of $25,000, and transactions under public utility tariffs (charges for delayed payment or discounts for early payment).

Finance charges

The most important section of the act is that dealing with the determination of finance charges. Before the act was passed, thousands of borrowers and buyers of merchandise on credit had been kept in the dark as to the true or actual interest rates they were paying. The interest or service charge was stated "in the fine print," but salesmen or lenders in most instances made no effort to enlighten the customer or borrower about the details. For example, a person borrowing $1,000 and paying $60 interest on that amount (added onto the note at the outset) for one year, assumed he was paying 6 percent for the money borrowed. Such an impression was erroneous. The $60, tacked on to the loan amount, brought the total to $1,060, a sum to be repaid in twelve equal monthly installments. But over the one-year period, because his monthly payments constantly reduced the loan, the borrower had the use, on the average, of only about one-half of the $1,000; so that the $60 charge in this instance became an effective true interest rate of 11 percent.

The actual provisions for determination of finance charges, as set forth in the act, are outlined in the following language:

> DETERMINATION OF FINANCE CHARGE
>
> Sec. 106. (a) Except as otherwise provided in this section, the amount of the finance charge in connection with any consumer credit transaction shall be determined as the sum of all charges, payable directly or indirectly by the person to whom the credit is extended, and imposed directly or indirectly by the creditor as an incident to the extension of credit, including any of the following types of charges which are applicable:
>
> (1) Interest, time price differential, and any amount payable under a point, discount, or other system of additional charges.
>
> (2) Service or carrying charge.
>
> (3) Loan fee, finder's fee, or similar charge.
>
> (4) Fee for an investigation or credit report.
>
> (5) Premium or other charge for any guarantee or insurance protecting the creditor against the obligor's default or other credit loss.

The act is not merely advisory; it imposes penalties. Anyone who fails to comply with certain requirements of the act is subject to a fine of not more than $5,000, or imprisonment for not more than one year, or both.

The act spells out the obligation of the creditor to include, in each account billing, where a finance charge is imposed on the unpaid balance: (1) the outstanding balance at the beginning of the statement period; (2)

the amount and date of each extension of credit, or identification and amount of any additional goods purchased; (3) the total amount credited to the account in the period; (4) the itemized amount of any finance charge added during the period, and the actual percentage rate it represented; and (5) the entire balance at the end of the statement period.

Also included are specific requirements for disclosure on sales and consumer loans not under open-end credit plans.

Credit cards are also covered with an injunction that "no credit card shall be issued except in response or application therefor." (This does not apply to cards sent in renewal of expiring ones.) The liability of the holder of a credit card for its unauthorized use is clarified, and penalties for fraudulent use of cards to obtain goods or services with retail value totaling $5,000 or more are set down: a fine of not more than $10,000, or imprisonment for not more than five years, or both.

Chapter three of the act is devoted to false and misleading advertising of credit.

The purpose of the legislation is to eliminate certain glaring abuses in the extension and the advertising of credit and of time-financed purchases, which had become all too common. The act is not, however, an arid aggregation of protective measures. It offers as well some exceedingly valuable information for consumers. First, the act alerts individuals to the need to know the annual percentage rate applying to each extension of credit. Armed with this information, an individual can reject a contract where interest appears excessive, and can shop elsewhere for more favorable terms.

Credit card safeguards

The section covering credit cards is particularly valuable. A few years back, some card issuers would put thousands of their plastic rectangles into the mail, addressed to people who were presumably credit-worthy. Many of these cards, however, never reached the persons to whom they were addressed, but were snatched out of mail boxes or garbage cans, and with forged signatures were used to buy goods or services until the persons unlawfully using the cards were apprehended and the cards blacklisted. Now the indiscriminate mailing of cards to those who have not requested them is not permitted; and loss to the cardholder if his card is dishonestly used is limited to $50, after the issuer has been notified of its loss or theft.

The provisions for disclosure in advertising are equally important. For example, it is now necessary, if credit is offered, to advertise not only the amount of down payment required in a particular transaction, but the number, amount, and timing of payments required to complete the contract; and the true, annual percentage rate charged.

Another provision in the act gives the consumer the right of cancellation, within three days, of a credit transaction arranged to provide a home improvement that is not covered by a first loan or mortgage. For instance, if you plan to add a porch to your house and the contractor takes a lien or mortgage on your home as security for payment, you have three days during which you may cancel the contract. The contractor (creditor) must give you written notice of your right to cancel, and you, in turn, if you decide you do not want the contract, must notify him in writing. Before this provision, the contractor could move in at once, begin work, and you would have been without recourse.

The latest piece of legislation aimed at protecting the consumer, Fair Credit Billing, was signed into law on October 29, 1974, and became effective one year after that date.

The new law, which amends Truth in Lending, provides consumers with a legal platform from which they can talk back to creditors' computers and defend themselves in the meantime, and restricts waiver-of-defense in the use of credit cards. Creditors are required to disclose fully these billing-complaint and waiver-of-defense rights.

Under this law, if a customer believes a billing error has been made, he or she must make the complaint known to the creditor in writing within sixty days of billing. The creditor must acknowledge receipt of the complaint within thirty days and has ninety days to resolve the problem. Any creditor failing to comply automatically forfeits the right to collect the amount in dispute as well as any finance charges, so long as the total amount to be forfeited does not exceed $50. During the period in which the billing error is being resolved, the creditor is forbidden from dunning the customer in any way. Threatening to make, or making, an adverse credit report on the consumer is also prohibited during this period.

Another Truth in Lending amendment resulting from the new legislation requires anyone selling an item that calls for four or more payments to state explicitly in all advertising the amount that is added on to the price of the item in lieu of interest. This protects consumers from misleading advertisements claiming that you can pay for an item in interest-free installments, when interest charges have been hidden in the form of higher prices.

There are, indeed, wide variations in the cost of credit for identical principal sums, either borrowed in cash, or defined as the immediate delivered cost of merchandise. You are obviously entitled to full and accurate disclosure as to the total cost and interest rate of the contract; and to compare interest and finance charges offered with those provided by other legitimate consumer credit suppliers serving the same consumer market. That is what truth in lending is all about.

State laws differ

The Truth in Lending Act is significant in another way. It highlights the fact that each state has its own law defining what rates of interest constitute usury, and its own distinctions in rates and conditions for borrowing to raise money for financing the purchase of goods and services, and for home mortgages. There may be one rate for personal loans, another legal rate for consumer goods financing, and still another official rate, or ceiling, for home mortgages.

Because many personal loan companies, finance companies, and mortgage-lending institutions do business in many states or nationwide, there exists a growing opinion that the rates and conditions under which these various credit transactions are handled should be uniform, and under national rather than state legislation. Such uniformity in credit practice may seem a logical goal, but it will be difficult to achieve because of the variations in existing usury laws and debt limits on personal loans in the states. Tennessee, for example, has a 10 percent legal limit on interest rates. If inflation continues and general interest rates go higher, how will the citizens of Tennessee be able to borrow money or buy goods "on time," when credit is extended in other states at 12 percent? Sources of credit will not willingly lend at 10 percent in one state if they can earn 2 percent more elsewhere.

A long-term goal might appear to be a national uniform Consumer Credit Act, picking up where the Truth in Lending Act leaves off.

CHAPTER 14

Protecting Your Credit Rating

About 40 percent of all Americans still buy nothing they cannot pay for in cash. They pay all their bills promptly—often on the day received—and would far rather get along without a television set, a washing machine, or a stereo system than buy one on time.

This group of dedicated cash customers, however, is a constantly shrinking one. It lost adherents in 1939 when Macy's, one of America's leading retail merchants, stopped selling for cash only and made available deferred-payment plans, allowing eight to thirty-six months to pay. In the years since then, more and more Americans have come to regard the use of credit as the most desirable way to make purchases.

There are now more than 120 million people in the United States almost continuously making payments on installment contracts for cash, goods, or services; and a representative family will on the average spend annually at least $500 more than its income for the first twenty years of marriage, making up the difference by borrowing.

Credit standing not secret

Good or bad, your credit-worthiness is almost a matter of public record. The extension of so much credit to so many people makes it essential that lenders of money and those agencies that finance goods and services know whom they are dealing with, and be able to screen out undesirables.

Accordingly, there has arisen across the land a network of agencies that constantly checks on personal credit to keep its records up-to-date. Today's sober, solvent, and dependable householder may become tomorrow's bad risk; so detection of danger in credit status is almost as important as a correct appraisal of credit-worthiness at the opening of any new account.

If you apply for credit at a department store, bank, or finance or loan company, or for a mortgage at a savings bank or savings and loan association, you are going to be investigated, and the probing party will have access to several sources of information about your financial standing and reliability.

If you have ever overdrawn at your bank, there is probably a record of it. If you have done it frequently, there may be a special memo in the bank's file about you. If you have taken ninety days to pay department store bills you may have a doubtful rating, difficult to erase. If you drag out payments on an oil company credit card, you will get the standard letters, be billed for interest, and possibly even have your card canceled. That too will go on your record. If you fail to pay your gas or electric bill, the utility company will cut off service and

How Consumer Installment Debts Are Rising

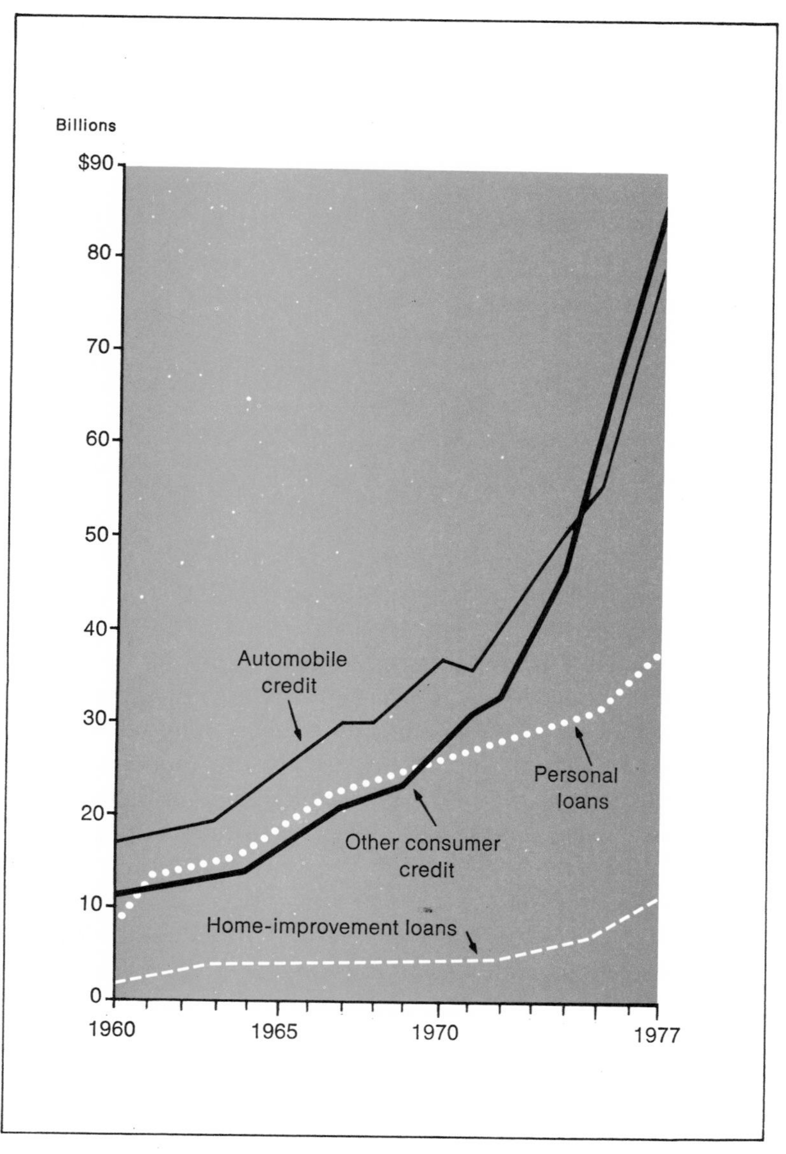

Sources: Federal Reserve Board, National Consumer Finance Association

What Consumers Owe

(in billions of dollars)

Type of Credit	*1977*
Total Consumer Credit	*$260.7*
Installment Credit, Total	*$216.6*
Automobile	79.4
Other Consumer Goods	85.3
Home Improvement	12.9
Personal Loans*	39.0
Noninstallment Credit, Total	*$44.1*
Single-Payment Loans	15.8
Charge Accounts**	13.5
Service Credit	14.8

*Data available only for commercial banks and finance companies.

**In addition to retail charge accounts, includes service station and miscellaneous credit card accounts and home heating oil accounts.

Source: Federal Reserve Board

will remember your delinquency years after you have paid up and had the service restored. Finally, if you have had a car repossessed, had judgments lodged against you, or, worst of all, had a bankruptcy action, your credit standing will be sullied, and your negative history can haunt you in all subsequent requests for credit, even though you may later become a millionaire.

Almost every significant delay or failure to pay indebtedness becomes part of your credit history and affects your rating. These lapses may become visible in a total interchange system, national in scope. If you leave a telephone bill unpaid in Bridgeport, Connecticut, you may have difficulty getting service installed in Omaha, Nebraska, until you settle the Bridgeport account. Exchange of credit information among regional telephone companies is standard operating procedure.

Equally, if you have not repaid a bank loan in Baltimore and apply for another in Seattle, you are not likely to get it. Inquiry about you through a correspondent eastern bank or by reference to a credit bureau or clearinghouse will reveal your default.

Credit investigators

Dun and Bradstreet has been renowned for decades for its credit investigations and reports of corporations and individuals; and, for a fee, Bishop's Service can prepare an extensive character and financial appraisal on almost any individual, regardless of his place of residence.

The super source of credit information, however, is Associated Credit Bureaus. This is really a trade organization, not a credit bureau. It has 1,900 members throughout the United States who assemble credit data and make it available to their subscribing members—banks, insurance companies, retail stores, finance companies, mortgage lending agencies, oil companies, travel bureaus, government agencies, police departments, and professional persons. On request of a subscriber, any independent local bureau will supply a report on a credit applicant for a moderate fee: an oral in-file report costing least; an updated oral report costing twice as much; and a written up-to-date report costing over three times as much.

Associated Credit Bureaus members comprise in fact a vast clearinghouse for gathering, updating, evaluating, and supplying accurate credit reports about individuals anywhere in the United States. Bureau members have assembled credit information on probably close to half of all Americans. Many people have no idea that so extensive and informed an organization even exists. With increased sophistication in microfilm, computerized and automatic data processing, storing, and retrieving, this financial reporting is becoming swifter and more comprehensive each day.

The largest bureau member is probably Credit Information Corporation of New York, serving a population of about 15 million people in the New York metropolitan area. This bureau has an estimated 1,500 subscribers—stores, lending institutions, insurance companies, and service organizations—and could probably muster useful financial data on at least 6 million people who reside in the area.

So when you casually fill out charge account forms in a department store, or a loan application at a bank or finance company, do not think that you can secure an accommodation to which you are not entitled. Through the network of bureau members, data concerning your history, your habits, your income level, and your tendencies with respect to assumption of debt and payments thereon can be promptly transmitted by letter, telephone, or teletype to confirm or disprove any statements you may make in your application for credit.

If an unshaven, somewhat sloppy-looking man walks into an exclusive store on Madison Avenue and seeks to open a charge account and to buy a $250 cashmere coat and take it with him, a telephone call to Credit Information Corporation will give the store the information and the assurance it needs to accept or reject the charge account and the order. The call may reveal that the would-be customer is a successful artist, lives in an $80,000 home in Westport, Connecticut, has an account at a leading bank, and satisfactorily maintains charge accounts with seven other New York stores.

Credit reporting

Of the 215 million people in the United States, more than 50 percent are on record for having made some purchase on credit, and credit reports on more than 35 million individuals are stored for instant recall in computer banks across the land.

Consumer Balance Sheet

(end-1977 estimates in billions of dollars)

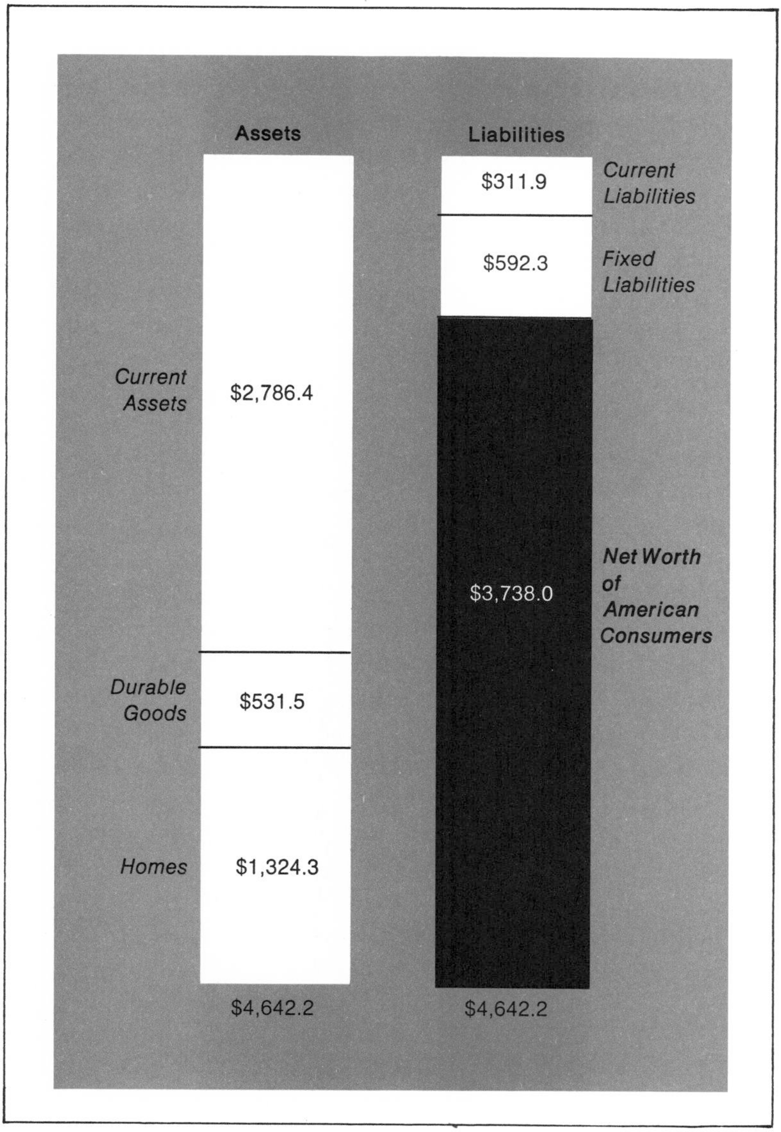

Assets		Liabilities	
		$311.9	*Current Liabilities*
		$592.3	*Fixed Liabilities*
Current Assets	$2,786.4	$3,738.0	*Net Worth of American Consumers*
Durable Goods	$531.5		
Homes	$1,324.3		
	$4,642.2	$4,642.2	

Note: "Current Assets" include savings, stocks, and other investments.

Sources: U.S. Department of Commerce, Federal Reserve Board, National Consumer Finance Association

The volume, extent, and availability of this personal credit information has created a myriad of problems, and brought to light many abuses and potential abuses in connection with consumer credit data which has been collected, tabulated, and made available. Everyone agrees as to the necessity of gathering information and establishing criteria to determine the granting or withholding of credit, insurance, or employment; but in this process there have arisen some real problems involving individual rights with respect to (1) disclosure of this information, (2) the unwarranted or unexplained withholding or denial of credit, insurance, or employment, (3) inclusion and dissemination of information that is inaccurate, incomplete, or false, and (4) failure to update—such as retaining adversely on the record a notation of a "judgment" lodged against an individual, even after the matter has been financially settled.

Further, it is important for individuals to be assured that legitimate data about their moral character and their capability and disposition to discharge obligations faithfully not be broadly circulated.

Finally, it has been regarded as proper, and indeed essential, that an individual have the right to look at and review the data about him or her which has been summarized by a credit bureau; and have corrected, amended, or updated any report that does not give a true current picture, or has unfairly resulted in a denial of credit due to errors in fact or because of conditions which have not been properly verified or updated.

Accordingly, the Fair Credit Reporting Act, which became effective on April 25, 1971, has been acclaimed as a much needed step in defining the responsibilities of credit agencies and placing upon them the burden of disclosure of personal credit data to any individual who may feel that his credit status has been misrepresented or that credit accommodation has been improperly denied or restricted because of a report made by a credit agency or bureau.

The language of the Fair Credit Reporting Act summarizes its intentions quite well in Section 602:

"(2) An elaborate mechanism has been developed for investigating and evaluating the credit worthiness, credit standing, credit capacity, character, and general reputation of consumers.

"(3) Consumer reporting agencies have assumed a vital role in assembling and evaluating consumer credit and other information on consumers.

"(4) There is a need to insure that consumer reporting agencies exercise their grave responsibilities with fairness, impartiality, and a respect for the consumer's right to privacy....

"(b) It is the purpose of this title to require that consumer reporting agencies adopt reasonable procedures for meeting the needs of commerce for consumer credit, personnel, insurance, and other information in a manner which is fair and equitable to the consumer, with regard to the confidentiality, accuracy, relevancy, and proper utilization of such information in accordance with the requirements of this title."

Credit bureaus

Before reciting the specific steps consumers may take in defense of their credit, or in correction of errors in reporting or disclosure, it is appropriate to examine the methods by which individual credit data is gathered, evaluated, and disseminated by representative agencies.

Few businesses are easier to enter than credit service. You do not need a license from a city or state, or any specific business credential or background to establish a credit bureau. Just rent an office, put a sign on the door, have a telephone installed, and begin soliciting customers. Further, there are no rigid criteria; so you may gather credit data from many sources and you are not held to accuracy. It is perfectly possible for a bureau to give out false information.

In practice, however, the trend is definitely toward larger credit bureaus, regional in coverage. Size and resources are increasingly important to assure: (1) capability in assembling credit data, constantly revising it and updating it as people move, die, get divorced, or go broke; and (2) the use of extensive data-processing equipment. Subscribers to a credit service seek not only dependable financial reporting but instant evaluations by telephone or teletype. Generally subscribers pay an annual membership fee to the credit bureaus they engage, plus a service charge for each inquiry they make. These fees are the life blood of the credit agencies and big bureaus in metropolitan centers generate large annual gross incomes.

Altogether, credit bureaus have some sort of file on over 105 million Americans. The biggest agencies are in New York and Chicago but there are substantial ones in all major cities. Most are linked by membership in the national trade association, Associated Credit Bureaus, of Houston, Texas.

Representative is the Chicago Credit Bureau, which reports on over 4 million individual residents in its metropolitan area of 400 square miles. It is believed that this Chicago bureau has over 2,000 subscribers, each of whom pays an annual $25 for membership and a stated fee for each inquiry. Getting a report on an out-of-town customer may require cooperation with a bureau in another city, and cost $2.50 per inquiry. Local reports cost less. The Chicago bureau, in common with other big city agencies, is involved in extensive interbureau reporting, which may account for 15 percent of its approximately 2 million inquiries in a single year.

The most significant development in the industry is no doubt TRW Credit Data, a computerized credit bureau, with a memory bank in California that can print out profiles on 40 million Americans. This "instant rating" is delivered to subscribing retail, insurance, and financial establishments. Also, a salesclerk can push a button at one of the 50,000 TRW Data Systems terminals across the country and get a "flashback" of credit acceptance or rejection after putting in a customer's name, address, and amount of the sale.

Your credit record may be among the millions stored in the TRW Credit Data memory bank. If you wish to obtain a printout of your credit profile, you may apply for it on a form available upon telephone or written request to the regional office of TRW Credit Data nearest you. The addresses and telephone numbers of these offices are: 1761 West Katella Avenue, Anaheim, California 92804, (714) 776-6580; 6022 West Touhy Avenue, Chicago, Illinois 60648, (312) 775-8500; and 20 Just Road, Fairfield, New Jersey 07006, (201) 575-8740.

Rating systems

Credit bureaus and retail stores vary in their methods of assessing applicants for credit. Some merely gather pertinent individual data; others have developed sophisticated rating systems. Where ratings are made, evaluations often depend on these eight factors: (1) your occupation; (2) how long you have held your present job; (3) where you live; (4) how long you have lived there; (5) your marital status; (6) your weekly earned income; (7) your bank accounts; and (8) any acceptable credit you have already established.

In the calculation of your credit-worthiness, your occupation is an important factor. As many as 275 vocations may be tabulated for credit screening purposes.

The best credit risks are considered to be business

A Sample Consumer Credit Report

This is the type of report furnished by TRW Credit Data in response to a consumer's request to see the information that has been compiled about his credit transactions. TRW Credit Data is a part of the vast TRW corporation, which operates in the fields of spacecraft and propulsion, energy-related products, tools and bearings, and automotive components, as well as electronics and computer-based services. The Credit Data system collects and distributes reports on consumers to suppliers of credit. A consumer whose credit history is among the 40 million recorded by TRW Credit Data can obtain a transcript of his report by paying a $4 fee, unless he applies within 30 days after having been denied credit, in which case there is no charge. The TRW files cover consumers in and around Sacramento, San Francisco, Anaheim, Los Angeles, San Diego, Las Vegas, Reno, Tulsa, Chicago, Detroit, Buffalo, Rochester, Syracuse, New York City, northern New Jersey, and Baltimore.

TRW® CREDIT DATA

James H. Doe
234 Anywhere Street
U. S. A. 84760

100 Anywhere
U. S. A. 74653
(000) 123-4566

DATE December 9, 1974

Dear Consumer:

In response to your recent request, under the name and address(es) you provided, the following is a transcript of the credit information maintained by TRW Credit Data:

If you disagree with any of the information shown below:

1. Please write your comments next to the item(s) in the "CONSUMER COMMENTS" column on the right. (Additional information regarding the item(s) you have marked may be supplied in the "ADDITIONAL COMMENTS" area on the reverse side of this form.)
2. If you have any comments, read the reverse side, sign and return this form in the enclosed envelope. Keep the CONSUMER COPY for your records.

Page 1

	CONSUMER COMMENTS
PAID SATISFACTORY ACCT REPORTED IN 4/74 BY SECURITY PACIFIC NATL BANK --CHECK GUARANTEE ACCT--CREDIT LIMIT $500--REVOLVING TERMS--ACCT OPENED IN 6/73--ACCT #140085399	
OPEN ACCT REPORTED IN 8/74 BY WELLS FARGO BANK--AUTO CONTRACT--ORIGINAL AMOUNT $5300--FOR 36 MONTHS--ACCT OPENED IN 8/74--ACCT #340500155	
PAID SATISFACTORY ACCT REPORTED IN 7/72 BY BANK OF AMERICA--AUTO CONTRACT--ORIGINAL AMOUNT $3000--FOR 36 MONTHS--ACCT OPENED IN 11/70--ACCT #623534279	
CLOSED ACCT REPORTED IN 9/74 BY SECURITY PACIFIC NATL BANK--CHECK GUARANTEE ACCT--CREDIT LIMIT $500--REVOLVING TERMS--ACCT OPENED IN 8/72--ACCT #568002006	
INQUIRY BY WELLS FARGO BANK IN 8/74	
OPEN ACCT REPORTED IN 6/72 BY BENEFICIAL FINANCE- ORIGINAL AMOUNT $2100--FOR 36 MONTHS--ACCT OPENED IN 6/72--ACCT #7523105	
** END OF REPORT**	
MAILED TO:	

Any item(s) you have marked will be investigated by contacting the source of the information. We will notify you, by mail, of the results of this investigation and changes, if any, made to our file. If for any reason we have not contacted you within three weeks, please call us at the number listed above, collect, if out of your toll free area.

CD-102 (6-74)

RETURN TO TRW CREDIT DATA *(IF ANY COMMENTS)*

executives who are customarily sensitive about their community standing and financial reputation. Next come accountants, who are presumed to be particularly prudent in financial matters. Retail store managers are high on the ladder; so are certain professionals—doctors, dentists, engineers, and architects—who are usually in high income brackets. Lawyers and judges are credit-worthy but are reputed to be a little slower in paying.

Military officers are among the preferred risks, and ahead of policemen, firemen, and bus and truck drivers. Public officials and clergymen are a little lower on the scale, not because they are less responsible but because of their lower incomes as compared with their generally high living standards. Salesmen, carpenters, plumbers, and janitors are down the line.

The least attractive risks from the standpoint of the professional lender include certain theatrical people and those whose employment tends to be more sporadic and whose incomes are less dependable: waitresses, maids, miners, musicians, bartenders, elevator operators, longshoremen, painters, and migratory workers.

In assessing the factor of job tenure, if you have been working in the same place for seven years, you get a top rating; two to five years, a lower rating; and less than two years, the lowest rating. Regarding your residence, you get the maximum rating if you own your own home; a lower rating if you rent an apartment or live with a relative; and the lowest rating if you rent a room or live in a trailer. The longer you have resided at your present address, the more stable you are considered to be. Five years of continued residence is adequate for a prime rating.

If you are married or widowed, you are regarded as stable. A single female is rated better than a single male; and a divorced female is considered to be far more

General Benchmarks for Credit-Worthiness

OCCUPATION

The following rating of various occupations is not fixed or absolute, but rather a composite profile derived at random from the lending experience of diverse suppliers of consumer credit. In evaluating occupation as a factor in credit-worthiness, the accent is on high and dependable income and status in a community. Based on a descending scale with a top rating of 10 points, the categories provide an indication of those in our society who have been found to be relatively more likely to meet their obligations promptly and not to incur debt beyond their capacity (or intention) to repay.

Group I (10 Points)
Top business executives, trustees, financial officers, senior military officers, accountants, doctors, dentists, and architects.

Group II (9 Points)
Public school teachers, professors, laboratory and university scientists, engineers, most clerical personnel (stenographers, bookkeepers, file clerks), postal employees, and civil service clerks.

Group III (8 Points)
Farmers, fishermen, carpenters, cabinetmakers, and railway and utility employees.

Group IV (7 Points)
Members of the clergy, nurses, dental assistants, printers, lithographers, newspaper and book editors, government officials, and skilled factory workers.

Group V (6 Points)
Lawyers, policemen, firemen, sanitation employees, construction workers, truck and bus drivers, and noncommissioned military personnel. (Note: Lawyers are given this lower credit status not on a solvency scale but because they may find legal loopholes in their contracts of obligation.)

Group VI (5 Points)
Authors, free-lance writers and artists, professional athletes, established actors (TV, screen, radio), dancers, and singers.

Group VII (4 Points)
Building and apartment custodians, tailors, barbers, plasterers, masons, and unskilled factory workers.

Group VIII (3 Points)
Bartenders, lawn and grounds caretakers, car, truck and trailer mechanics, appliance repairmen, and boatyard workers.

Group IX (2 Points)
Domestic help, house painters, musicians, novice actors, waitresses, and carhops.

Group X (1 Point)
Migratory workers, house-to-house salesmen, professional gamblers, cab drivers, bellhops, and busboys.

OTHER CRITERIA

Job tenure: If you have been working in the same place for 7 years, you get a top rating in this category (7 points); 2 to 5 years, 5 points; and less than 2 years, 2 points.

Residence: You get the top rating (6 points) if you own your own home; 3 points if you rent an apartment or live with a relative; and only 1 point if you rent a room or live in a trailer. The longer you have resided at your present address, the more credit-stable you are considered to be (migrants and wanderers are hard to keep track of). Five years in one place is all you need for a prime rating (6 points).

Marital status: If you are married or widowed, you get 6 points. A single female is rated better than a single male (4 points compared to 3); and a divorced female is more desirable as a credit risk, receiving 2 points, than either a divorced or separated male, who earns just 1 point.

Weekly earnings: Over $250 a week receives the maximum rating of 6 points; $200 down to $100 scores 4 points; $100 to $80, 3 points; $80 to $60, 1 point; and incomes below $60 are not rated.

Liquid assets: If you have a checking and a savings account, you rate 6 points; and as between the two, a savings account is worth 3 points, 50 percent more than a checking account, which is worth 2 points on the credit scale.

Credit references: You score points for the kind of credit profile you have built up. Six points are given for American Express, Diners Club, or Carte Blanche credit cards. If you have a gas credit card and department store cards in good standing, they are worth 5 points. The arbiters of consumer credit think little of a finance company or jewelry store reference, rating you just 1 point for this, either because the purchase is "frivolous" or because you evidence meager resources.

SCORING

Using the above benchmarks for ratings, with maximums of 10 points for vocation, 7 points for job tenure, 6 each for type and length of residence, marital status, weekly earnings, liquid assets, and credit references, the maximum total is 53. In this hypothetical evaluation system, you fail if your total is below 21 but are solidly welcome with 42 or more points. Under such a rating system, many combinations may qualify you for credit; but remember that credit is denied to many persons who appear to merit it by the above or similar credit approval methods.

desirable as a credit risk than either a divorced or separated male.

Those who earn over $400 a week receive a top rating in the income category, and those with lesser earnings rate lower. Credit-worthiness is, as you see, a composite of your ability and your disposition to pay.

In rating your liquid assets, the bureaus favor you if you have both a checking and a savings account; and if you have just one of these, a savings account is worth more than a checking account on your credit altimeter.

Finally you score points for the kinds of credit references you have built up. To score high, have two gas credit cards or two department store cards.

Under this type of rating system, many combinations may make you acceptable; but you should be aware that credit is denied to thousands of applicants who really merit receiving it and favorable ratings are accorded to thousands of persons who do not deserve them.

At best, credit rating is an imperfect science and those who are casualties of the system have legitimate complaints.

On occasion women have been denied credit in the same amount and at the same interest rate as obtained by men in similar circumstances. This matter has been spotlighted by the feminist movement, and credit evaluations are being equalized as the result of two recently enacted pieces of legislation.

The first prohibits sex discrimination against women when they are seeking a mortgage, and requires that a woman's income be taken into account when a couple is applying for a mortgage. There have been situations in which a husband earning $18,000 a year and a wife earning $15,000 a year were denied a $45,000 mortgage on a home, not because $33,000 in combined income was inadequate to support such an indebtedness, but because the loan officer thought that the woman might lose her income (and erode the credit base for the mortgage) if she became pregnant.

The second new law, effective as of October 29, 1975, entitles married women to establish credit under their own names rather than their husbands' and allows them to keep the credit ratings they had established prior to marriage. The act also equalizes borrowing standards for women with those for men, prohibits discrimination in lending to minorities, and additionally protects all consumers against unfair credit billing.

Correcting errors

What recourse do you have if you believe that you may have been denied credit, insurance, or employment because of inaccurate or outdated information?

Your first step should be to contact your local credit bureau, which undoubtedly has a complete dossier on you. Begin your search for this firm by looking in the yellow pages of your telephone book under the heading "Credit Bureaus" or "Credit Reporting Agencies." When you find the heading, look for an entry that is obviously concerned with consumer credit, such as "Credit Bureau, Inc., member of Associated Credit Bureaus."

If the yellow pages do not provide the information you seek, ask an official at your bank to tell you where your credit file may be located. If this source of information also fails to help you, inquire at your local Better Business Bureau or the nearest Federal Trade Commission office.

Under the Fair Credit Reporting Act, you may send in to the credit bureau (once you have located it) a form requesting either a personal or telephone interview concerning the data in your file. You may examine your file in the credit reporting agency at any time for a small fee. If your file has resulted in a refusal of credit, you have the right to examine the file without charge.

If the report is correct and your rating is excellent, you may request the credit bureau to so state in writing and thus, perhaps, expedite your acceptance for a loan, merchandise credit, insurance, employment, or a credit card.

If a cloud on your acceptability has appeared because of improper data in the report, you may insist that (1) any item over seven years old (except judgments or bankruptcy) be deleted; (2) any erroneous or untrue item be removed; (3) a claim at one time lodged against you be removed, if it has been paid off; (4) unsubstantiated or undocumented claims (such as from deceased creditors) be erased; and (5) notification be sent to anyone who received a credit report on you within the previous six months, informing that recipient of any deletion or significant change made in your report as a result of reinvestigation.

If you contest an item in your file, it must be reinvestigated and deleted in event the item is found to be false or unable to be verified. If a contested item is verified, you have the right to insert a statement in the file giving your side of the dispute.

If a company desires an investigative consumer report on your character or general reputation, the company is obligated to report this fact to you by mail within three days after such a report is first requested. This is your alert. The law requires that the agency shall, upon your request and proper identification, clearly and completely disclose to you the substance and nature of all data about you in its files.

In your behalf, the Fair Credit Reporting Act limits the furnishing of a consumer report to these circumstances:

(1) in response to the order of a court having jurisdiction;

(2) in accordance with the written instruction of the consumer to whom the credit relates;

(3) in response to a person who intends to use the information in connection with the extension or collection of a consumer credit account, or for employment purposes, or in connection with the underwriting of insurance involving the consumer;

(4) in connection with determination of a consumer's eligibility for a license or other benefit granted by governmental responsibility; or

(5) in response to anyone who has a valid need for the information because of a business transaction involving the consumer.

The act contains several additional instructions and restrictions which are aimed at keeping this personal information as private as possible, and protecting individuals from unauthorized and improper disclosure thereof.

Maintaining your standing

If you get the credit you seek, it is up to you to maintain your standing by properly relating your indebtedness to your income. As a general rule, interest and principal reduction payments on consumer indebtedness should not exceed 20 percent of your disposable annual income. If the percentage rises to 25 or 30 percent, you are flirting with trouble.

Do not seek the longest repayment term available because it will cost considerably more in total interest and you will have nothing to fall back on if you get behind in your payments. For example, if you have a twenty-four-month car loan, you will get out of debt faster and pay less interest than for one running thirty-six months; and if you should get into a financial bind, you can stretch out the twenty-four-month loan into a longer contract, reducing monthly payments correspondingly.

Watch, too, buying on credit an item that involves many extra costs for its operation. You may be able to afford a modest motor boat on time payments, but remember that there will be high costs for fuel, insurance, maintenance, repairs, between-season storage, and rental of a berth at a marina or, more expensive still, a yacht club membership.

When you have any installment debt, punctuality and regularity of payments are essential to keep you in good standing. Pay credit card bills immediately, department store charge accounts by the tenth of the month; and other debts preferably at once but no later than the second notice. The third or fourth reminders mark you as a doubtful case, and a telephone call to prod you is a black mark.

If, for some reason, a payment has been so delayed that you receive a prodding telephone call, be sure to send the money at once. The most frequently uttered lie in the business world is the sentence, "The check is in the mail."

If you change your place of residence, advise all your creditors of your new address at once, so that notices may be properly delivered to you. Sometimes, even the most meticulous people overlook and miss a payment date; and if the reminder does not reach them, they may fall in arrears, without any intention to do so. When mailed notices are returned to lenders, their suspicion is aroused, because elusive debtors have been a chronic source of trouble to them.

Finally, never send as payment a check that bounces. This is a distress signal in the credit business, and will appear as a blot on your record, when an isolated delayed payment will not.

The way to maintain your credit standing is very simple: meet each and every payment promptly. As an extra measure, pay up a contract ahead of time once in a while; you may incidentally receive an interest refund as a bonus for doing so.

Unquestioned credit can bring a continuous flow of good things to you—so do not clog this financial pipeline to material well-being with any delinquency. Credit does not depreciate by use. Lenders do not fawn over affluent people with marvelous credit ratings who never have to borrow. Their favorite client is a solvent person with a good income who borrows continuously and pays promptly, using his or her credit to assemble a steadily growing inventory of useful and enjoyable assets, without deferring their acquisition until enough funds are saved up to make an all-cash payment.

Sale
$80

CHAPTER 15

How to Handle Overextended Credit

Although neither you nor a member of your family may ever go on a buying spree, piling up debts which cannot be met, few people are invulnerable to overextended credit. If you lose your job in a recession, or because of an accident or a long illness, you may find that you are faced with an array of overdue debts for charge accounts, credit card bills, mortgage interest, car purchase, and possibly a bank loan as well.

Troubles such as these may not beset you, but they are definitely on the increase. "By the end of this year (1974), as many as 10 families out of every 100 could find themselves overextended, compared with 3 in every 100 in 1973," stated Robert Gibson, president of the National Foundation for Consumer Credit, in August, 1974. Higher prices have been compelling people to resort to credit for purchases heretofore made with cash. Fear of runaway inflation and still higher prices has been causing many people to rush to make major purchases, rather than pay more for them a year hence. So they have been borrowing, accepting interest charges of 18 percent and not realizing that they are at, or already above, the debt ceiling that their incomes can comfortably support.

Warning signals in 1974-75 were declines in employment in the automobile and construction industries, lower prices for livestock in agricultural areas, and a steady decline in brokerage and investment banking revenues and in the values of common stocks (a part of the net worth of millions of people). Nevertheless, credit card balances rose about 25 percent in the first six months of 1975. The economic clouds cleared in 1976. Stocks rose, car sales zoomed, and new credit cards were being issued at an annual expanded rate of about 13 percent.

Further, solicitation of personal loans continues. Letters from banks remind clients that money is there, waiting for them to ask for a loan. Newspaper advertisements of banks and finance companies across the country still beckon you to come in and open an account, and to draw checks even when you have nothing in your account.

Perils of debt

There have always been perils attached to debt. Apart from inflation, recession, and possible unemployment, there are a number of other familiar causes for debtor jitters. First there is extravagant living beyond your income and buying more than you can afford, either for cash or on credit. A married man with four children is likely to be in debt for one-third of his married life, unless he receives large salary increases, or is the beneficiary of a substantial inheritance. A compulsive shopper

The Rise in Consumer Prices
(1967 = 100)

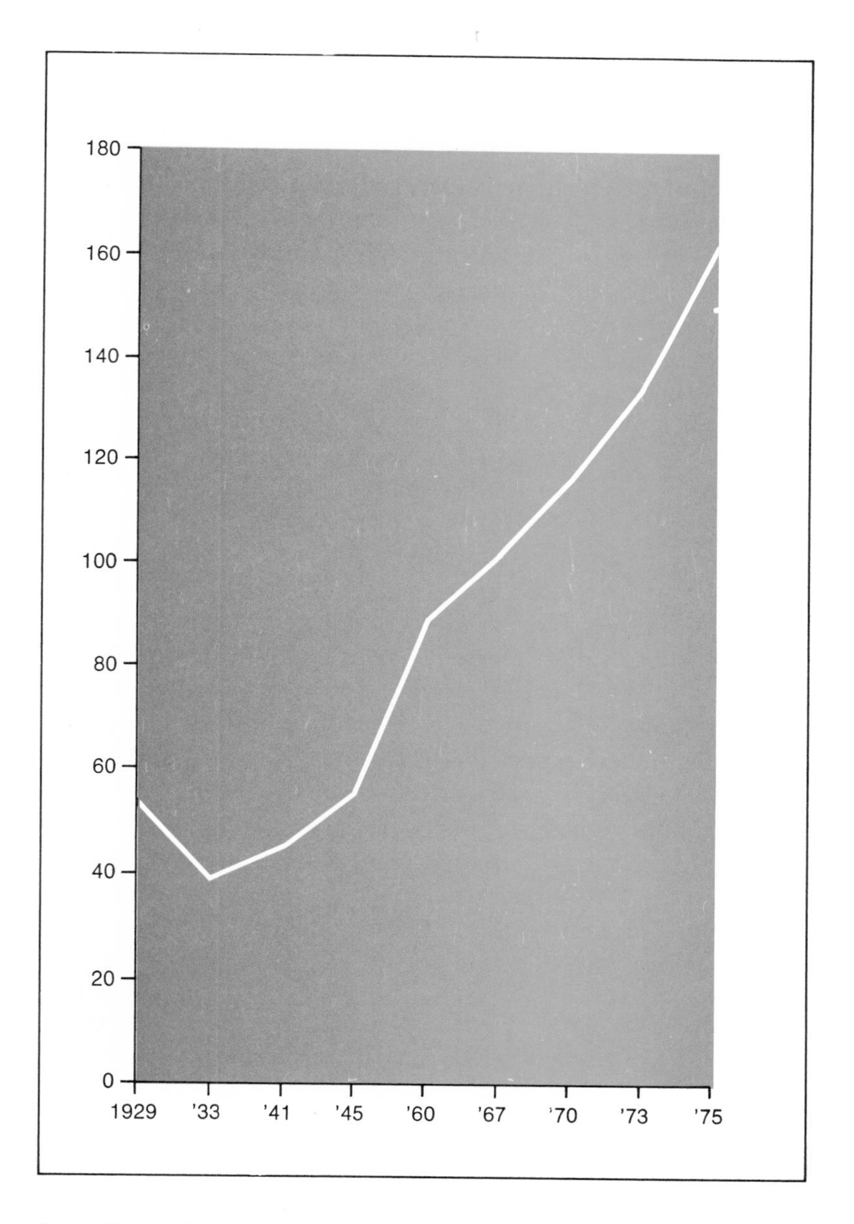

Source: Bureau of Labor Statistics

in the family can sink the financial ship; keeping up with the Joneses can have the same result. An alcoholic or a compulsive gambler in the family can torpedo any budget.

Marital difficulties can also create financial problems. A high percentage of home foreclosures is due to separations or divorces. Bill collectors swoop in when the husband stops paying for the clothing, jewelry, and furs a disgruntled wife may have bought out of spite.

Other credit difficulties have been caused by third-party holders of notes. If you bought a television set from an appliance dealer for, say, $400 and signed a time-payment contract, this credit instrument might have been sold to a finance company. If the television set proved to be defective, you might, in anger, have stopped paying the installments on your note. The finance company would have tried to collect the full payment specified in the contract (with interest) from you; and if it could not, it would have repossessed the television set. They had bought your note without reference to the quality of merchandise involved, and you owed them the money regardless of the condition or performance of the set.

This kind of sale of installment paper has worked hardships in many of the poorer areas of our cities. In such cases a low-income customer might be sold a cheap, defective, or even rebuilt radio, television set, or washing machine and then make a $20 down payment and leave the store with a coupon book calling for $20-a-month payments for the following eighteen months. If the item he purchased did not work, neither the unscrupulous merchant who sold him the dud, nor the finance company would help him.

To eliminate this type of credit problem, a new Federal Trade Commission ruling became effective in May 1976. The rule upsets the holder-in-due-course laws, introduced in the eighteenth century, requiring customers to honor their financial obligations to a third party, regardless of any argument with the vendor over faulty merchandise.

Under the new rule, if a consumer buys, say, a $300 washing machine from a merchant and signs an installment payment contract for it, and the merchant sells that obligation to a bank or finance company, then both the merchant and the financing agency may be held responsible if the merchandise proves defective. The vendor and the indirect lender together may be liable for all the money the consumer spent on his purchase.

The rule affects specifically bank and finance companies that lend money for the purchase of such consumer goods as automobiles, appliances, television sets, and so forth. However, it applies only when the lender has a contract, agreement, or other relationship with a vendor or dealer which makes the financing agency an indirect, or third-party, lender.

Creditors' remedies

Here is what will happen if you ever stop paying your debts, for whatever reason. First you will receive letters cajoling you into catching up on your payments. Then the communications will become threatening; next you will receive telephone calls about the matter and perhaps personal visits from collectors at your place of employment. Finally, you will receive a letter from a lawyer. Banks will be fairly courteous and considerate; personal loan companies more aggressive; and finance companies and used-car dealers are likely to harass you. And if you are in the clutches of a loan shark, you may find paint smears on your house, bricks thrown to break your windows, or telephone calls threatening harm to a member of your family. You may even get run off the road as you are driving, or be assaulted on the street.

Throughout most of the long history of moneylending, the transactions have been heavily weighted in favor of the lenders. For centuries before the Christian era debtors in default could be sold into slavery. A death penalty was not ruled out, but it was obviously less profitable than selling the live debtors. Antonio, in *The Merchant of Venice,* was to forfeit one pound of flesh nearest his heart as a penalty for his failure to repay a loan of 2,000 ducats. Debtors' prisons were part of the European scene for centuries.

We do not have prisons or death sentences for debtors anymore—although loan sharks sometimes use startling collection methods—but legal lenders still have an arsenal of remedies, depending on the amount and kind of loan and the various state laws, which increasingly have tended to make debt contracts more equitable.

Acceleration

A widely-used creditor's remedy is an acceleration clause in a consumer credit contract, whether for a cash loan or for merchandise. Under the Uniform Commercial Code provision, the acceleration takes the form of regarding the entire debt, including future installments, as due and payable upon default by the debtor, usually for nonpayment of principal or interest. The right of acceleration may be specified in either unsecured or secured loans.

Attorney's fees

Some states permit writing into the loan contract a clause stating that the debtor will pay attorney's fees if he defaults on the contract. The amount involved is usually a percentage of the amount in default, regardless of actual attorney fees incurred. This clause, found principally in small-loan contracts, is frowned on by many states.

Confession of judgment

By having a confession-of-judgment clause in a contract the debtor allows an attorney, chosen by the creditor, to appear in a court having jurisdiction, and to enter a judgment against the debtor at any time, even prior to any default, without notifying him. This clause is generally regarded as most unjust, and is prohibited in many states.

Security interest and repossession

A powerful clause used widely in merchandise installment contracts involves security interest and refers to the assignment of interest in personal property to secure payment of an obligation. It gives the right to the secured party, in event of default, to take possession of specified collateral without any judicial process, assuming this can be done without a breach of the peace. Even after such possession of collateral, if its sale brings less than the amount owed, there can be a deficiency judgment against the debtor. This is a clause most protective to the lender, and in various forms it is used in sales credit transactions.

Wage assignment and garnishment

A wage-assignment clause is quite severe and thoroughly unwelcome to debtors. It provides for assignment to the creditor of the right to collect a debtor's wages—all or a specified part—as security for, or in payment of, a debt. This clause enables the creditor to press his collection swiftly, without any discussion of the merits of the claim.

Many states place restrictions on wage-assignment clauses. Attachment harms debtors by creating a prior lien on money usually needed for living expenses; and some firms take a dim view of employees so deeply in debt as to have their wages attached.

Garnishment is a similar procedure and relates specifically to a court order demanding that an employer withhold part of an employee's compensation and pay such withholdings directly to, or for the account of, a creditor of the employee.

There is a wide assortment of state laws on garnishment and wage-withholding, covering duration and conditions and variously restricting garnishment to reasonable, and not confiscatory, percentages of compensation.

Other remedies

Other less frequently applied creditors' remedies include "cross collateral," a provision whereby assets of the debtor, in addition to the item purchased, may be included as security for completion of a sales contract.

A particularly drastic remedy is the enforcement of legal judgment against a debtor by seizure of his property (unless exempt from seizure by state statute) by a sheriff or marshal.

The foregoing indicates what you may have to face if you cannot pay your debts.

None of these remedies applies to all debts nor in all states; but you will probably find several of these provisions in any note you sign.

If you cannot pay

What then should you do, if you cannot pay on schedule, to avoid all the remedies available to your legitimate creditors, who may finally remove your refrigerator or tow away your car?

First of all, be completely candid. Do not tell creditors that you are going to send them money if you are not. Answer the doorbell and do not hide or run away. Then follow this program:

1. Maintain a calm attitude at all times.

2. Make a determined and immediate effort to cut down on all living expenditures.
3. Set up a priority schedule of debts; and aim to continue some sort of payment to the most demanding creditors.
4. Make an analysis and inventory of your assets available for conversion into cash to meet payments.
5. Arrange, if possible, a consolidation loan, so that you will owe money to only one place.
6. Arrange to compromise, adjust, modify, or stretch out payments to creditors if a consolidation loan will not pay them off in full.
7. Try to gain time. You will probably be able to meet your financial commitments if only you have enough time, perhaps by working overtime or moonlighting on a second job.

To review this program: Calmness is essential to your health and to making sound decisions. So use every technique you can to keep cool and unflappable.

On cutting down, there is much you can do quite painlessly. Use the car less; buy cheaper foods; do not purchase new clothes; stay home instead of taking an expensive vacation; cut down on beverages, cigarettes, and entertainment; do not purchase anything on credit.

Making priority decisions can also help you. You must pay utility bills, taxes, and rent or mortgage interest. Try to pay off club bills so you will not get "posted" there, with everyone talking about you and publicizing your difficulties. If you cannot pay up at the club, resign your membership.

Whenever you must delay payment, notify your creditor that you are temporarily "a little short" and assure him of your intention to pay as soon as you can. This will not make him happy, but it will keep him from taking instant and drastic action—and it will give you time.

The search for overlooked assets that can be sold may provide the solution to your problem. Old coins may be unearthed; a stamp collection may prove valuable; jewelry may be convertible into cash. A piece of furniture gathering dust in the basement may prove to be a valuable antique. You may be able, also, to increase the mortgage on your house, or borrow more on the market value of your car.

A consolidation loan can be very useful and can be obtained without difficulty from a bank, a personal loan company, or a credit union. To structure such a loan, you should present to the lending agency a complete schedule of your indebtedness and an accurate statement of your current income. The size of the consolidation loan will be geared to these figures. After the loan has been arranged, the lender may insist on sending checks directly to your creditors, lest you be tempted to do something else with the money. Your debt will then be all in one place and within your ability ultimately to discharge, over as long a period of months as you are able to negotiate. Your financial rehabilitation would be aided if you were to get rid of your credit cards, to remove the temptation to build new debts—and problems.

If the debts you have run up are too extensive to come under the shelter of the consolidation loan, you will have to discuss a special accommodation with each creditor. Offer some money on account, and the prospect of full payment within eighteen months. Most creditors will accept such evidence of your sincerity rather than start a lawsuit.

If your position is too desperate for any of the above-suggested remedies, then offer 75 cents on the dollar payable a year hence.

If all of the above approaches fail to solve your debt problems, you had best get a lawyer on a standby basis, to handle possible suits and prevent or limit garnishment of your salary or wages or an attachment of assets. Perhaps the lawyer can persuade your creditors to accept 50 cents on the dollar.

If this or any other compromise can serve to avoid bankruptcy, welcome it. Bankruptcy is a black mark against you. If you have hit rock bottom financially, bankruptcy will give you a little peace of mind and enable you to climb back up. But it will go down indelibly in your credit record. It is, however, to be preferred to ruining your life in a losing struggle against a mountain of debt. Bankruptcy will not give you a clean reputation but it will give you a clean slate, and substitute hope for despair.

NO DOWN PAYMENT
YOUR CREDIT GOOD HERE!
BUY NOW - PAY LATER
BILL
CLOSING DATE
REF. NO.
DATE
DEPT
ITEM
BALANCE

CHAPTER 16

Disturbing Levels of Credit

The overall monetary philosophy of the United States has gone through a remarkable series of changes in this century. During the first three decades, the existence of personal debt was still looked upon as a character defect. If you could not pay your bills, you were "weak" and needed "sound" counsel, supervision, and possible support from solvent (and smug) relatives and your church or a philanthropic institution. If you "got behind" in payments to the grocer, the coal man, the department store, or the family doctor, you were certain to be talked about—and not too charitably—even though your financial bind was due to a large family, an illness, or unemployment, not to mention more reprehensible causes: an extravagant wife, drunkenness, or trying desperately to keep up with the Joneses.

In the era before the Great Depression, mortgaging your home was regarded as a form of moral dereliction; many people who had inherited wealth would prefer a nervous breakdown to "invading principal"; not one individual in fifty qualified for, or could get, a personal loan at a bank; and using money for purchases of stocks in Wall Street was "gambling."

Long-term installment debt—four years to pay for an automobile, seven years to pay for a college education, and thirty years to pay off a home mortgage—all these credit extensions, commonplace now, were not available until the 1930s. House mortgages almost invariably ran for three to five years, without arrangements for reductions in principal amounts along the way; and 6 percent was almost always the interest rate.

One of the prime causes of the 1929-33 depression was the coming due of principal on a myriad of first-mortgage liens on homes and farms. It did not matter if the mortgagors could continue to pay the interest. The whole mortgage legally became due, and lenders, almost to a man, insisted on full payment or exercise of their right to foreclose, rather than arrange for an extension. In the cities, tens of thousands of individuals lost their homes not because they were improvident, but because they were unemployed and had to use for living expenses those personal resources they would otherwise have had available to pay off the $2,000, $3,000, or $5,000 owed on their mortgages. In a cluster of midwestern states, almost one-third of all the farm property was foreclosed in 1932 and 1933, mostly by insurance companies and savings banks that held the mortgages.

Then, too, tens of thousands of other individuals were wiped out in this period by the disastrous drops in common stock prices. The Dow Jones Industrial Average in 1932 reached a low of 42. Many eager, greedy, and probably insufficiently resourced individuals in this era

Where Consumers Obtain Installment Credit

(in millions of dollars)

	Outstanding Year-End 1973	*Outstanding Year-End 1977*
Total installment credit	$148,273	$216,557
Commercial banks	71,871	105,291
Finance companies	37,243	44,000
Credit unions	19,609	37,036
Retailers*	16,395	21,082
Others**	3,155	9,149
Automobile loans	51,274	79,414
Commercial banks	31,502	46,119
Finance companies	11,927	14,325
Credit unions	7,456	18,385
Others	389	585
Mobile home loans		
Commercial banks	8,340	8,862
Finance companies	3,378	3,109
Home-improvement loans	7,453	12,951
Commercial banks	4,083	6,473
Revolving credit		
Bank credit cards	6,838	14,262
Bank check credit	2,254	3,724
All other	68,736	91,193
Commercial banks	18,854	25,850
Personal loans	12,873	17,740
Finance companies	21,021	26,422
Personal loans	16,587	21,281
Credit unions	11,564	15,518
Retailers	16,395	21,082
Others	902	2,321

*Excludes 30-day charge credit held by retailers, oil and gas companies, and travel and entertainment companies.

**Mutual savings banks, savings and loan associations, auto dealers, and, in the case of home-improvement loans, finance companies.

Sources: Federal Reserve Board, National Consumer Finance Association

speculated dangerously in buying stocks on margin, putting up only 10 or 20 percent of their own money and borrowing the rest of the cost of a given stock purchase from their brokers.

One of the "darling" stocks of that period was Technicolor, owner of remarkable patents that brought life-like color to the motion picture screen. Technicolor's common stock sold as high as 100 in 1930 and as low as 1 in 1933. Suppose you had bought shares on 20 percent margin in 1930, when the issue was at 100—$2,000 of your money as a pledge against the total cost (excluding brokerage) of $10,000. When the stock fell to 80, you would have been wiped out, unless you could put up more collateral. If you had invested an additional $2,000, your total investment of $4,000 would have been lost when Technicolor plummeted below 60.

Less demanding conditions

The foregoing illustrations show the disasters of debt in an earlier time. Today indebtedness can still cause serious problems, even though the conditions for personal borrowing are more flexible and far less demanding than during the first third of this century. Most borrowers now understand that (1) you must have a dependable source of income if you are going to borrow; (2) that you should try to keep some cash in reserve; (3) that you should plan a program of repayment; and (4) that the amount you owe on a loan is not as important as how soon you must pay it back. If you agree to repay a loan of $20,000 twenty years from now, the contract may present no problem, but if you must repay even $2,000 by next Monday, you might be in an absolute financial panic.

Of all Americans living on a steady salary or wage, probably one out of three would have no liquid resources if he or she were to be unemployed for six months. That

Savings as a Percentage
Of Disposable Personal Income

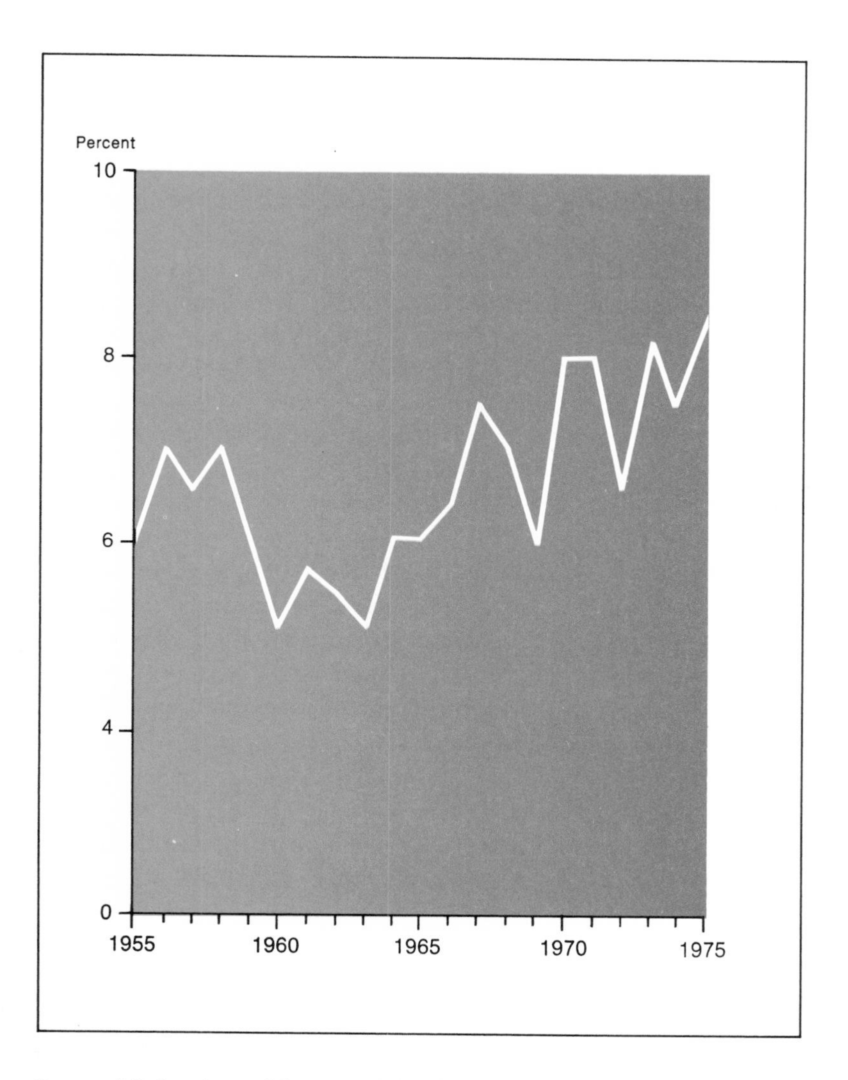

Sources: U.S. Department of Commerce, United States League of Savings Associations

is how closely most people live to their incomes. It suggests that if we were to have another depression, millions of people soon would be in financial trouble.

In the 1970s most Americans have a completely different viewpoint about debt from that prevailing in the 1930s. Debt, instead of being reprehensible and raising eyebrows, is now generally regarded as perfectly respectable. It enables us to have and enjoy goods and services months or even years before we could have them if we had to pay cash for them. A trip to Europe, a new car, a summer cottage, a new condominium apartment, dancing lessons, a coin collection, or a ski trip can be yours with only a modest down payment.

The economy of our country prospers by producing and selling things today that will not be fully paid for by the purchasers until two or three years, or more, have passed.

Will Rogers said in 1927 that the way to solve our traffic problem was to "keep all the cars that are not paid for off the road." If instant cash were to become the indispensable prerequisite for possession and use of all goods and services, the United States would very quickly suffer a severe economic depression.

Three stages

Taking a larger view of our national economic thinking, we have moved gradually through three stages. First, we sought to maintain a steady price level—by a gold standard, personal and corporate prudence, and governmental limitation on spending (balanced budgets). This was an era when thrift was the cardinal financial virtue, and it ended in 1933.

Next, our government sought to achieve rising price levels and general prosperity through expanded credit available at low interest rates. This phase flowered in 1946 with the passage of the Full Employment Act. At that time there was no stigma to debt at any level, if it fueled and maintained full employment.

Then we entered the third phase of our new economic euphoria—the growth syndrome of the 1960s. Each year was to exceed the preceding one in output of goods and services; and our total national well-being was to be judged by gains in that massive statistic of our time—Gross National Product. This expansion, too, took for granted big boosts in borrowing at all levels. Corporations could not expand their plants to assure all this additional output unless they borrowed money; the plowback of current earnings was not sufficient to finance the expansion. Individuals borrowed to buy more homes, furniture, appliances, and clothes. And now we have reached all-time highs in the various categories of debt.

Causes of peak debts

We have reached such altitudes of debt because employment and per capita incomes have long been in a steadily upward trend and because legislators have authorized—with full endorsement of their electorate—massive expenditures for military goods, social security, welfare, highways, agricultural supports (until 1974), war in Vietnam, military aid to other countries, and over $100 billion in nonmilitary aid to nations since 1944.

All this federal spending was paid for by massive additions to the national debt, serious loss of our gold reserves ($24.8 billion in 1948 and only $10.5 billion in 1971), and printing huge amounts of money (inflation). By 1974 the dollar had lost 76 percent of its 1939 purchasing power. The United States currently owes over $90 billion to foreign central banks and nations. We have already experienced two devaluations of the dollar and the decline of the dollar in relation to the deutsche mark, the yen, and the Swiss franc. A dollar was worth four deutsche marks in 1950 and less than two in 1978.

Ratio of Installment Debts To Disposable Income

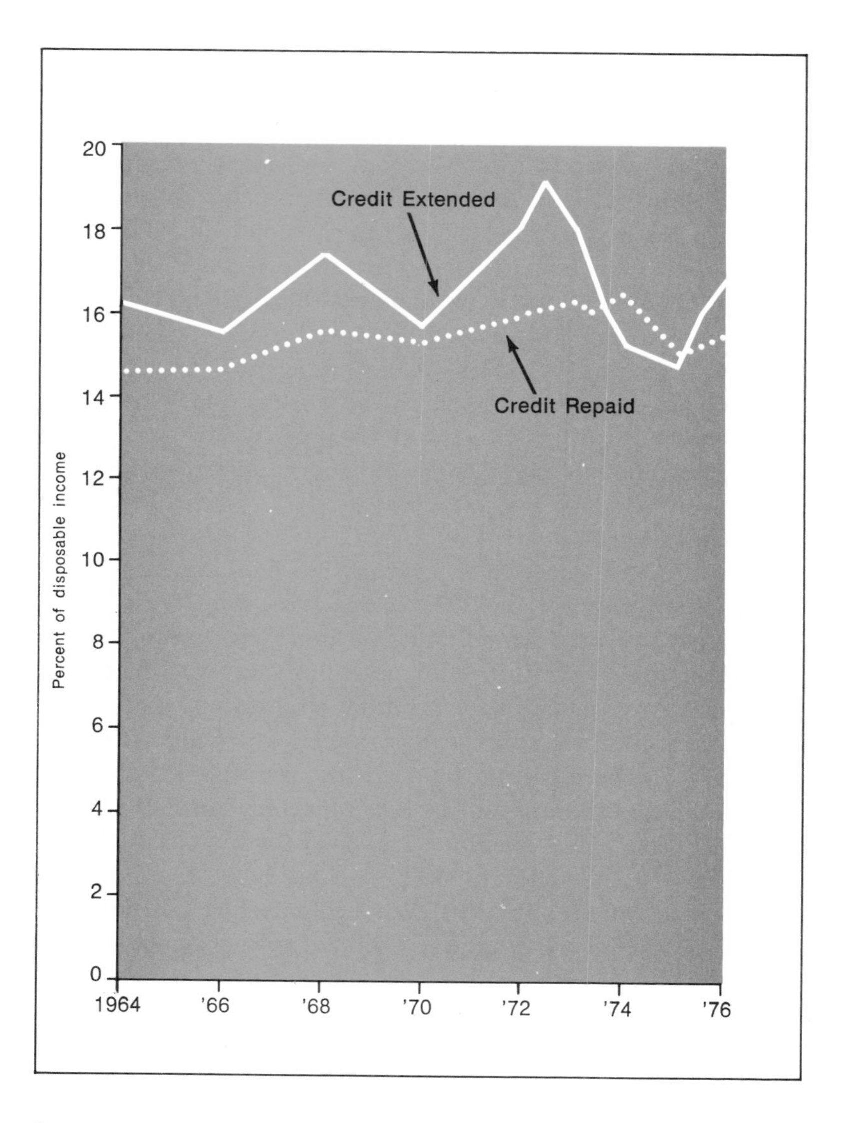

Sources: U.S. Department of Commerce, Federal Reserve Board, National Consumer Finance Association

Present debts appear to be at dangerous levels nationally and down the line to municipalities, corporations, and individuals. Moreover, we have had some warnings of serious trouble ahead. The U.S. National Bank of San Diego, with over $1 billion on deposit, failed in 1973 and required some $65 million in payments by the Federal Deposit Insurance Corporation and a sizable takeover of deposits and an infusion of capital by Crocker National Bank. In the spring of 1974, the Franklin National Bank, one of the largest commercial banks in the nation, got into a liquidity crisis and passed up the dividend on the stock of its holding company; trading in that issue was suspended on the over-the-counter market until an official earnings statement was prepared and made public. When it appeared, the statement revealed a loss of $65 million for the first five months of 1974. In 1975 Franklin was taken over by European-American bank. In 1978 the Citizens and Southern National Bank, the largest in Georgia, discontinued dividends which had been paid continuously since 1906.

And, of course, there was the earlier Penn Central debacle, the largest bankruptcy in the history of our nation. Penn Central was still losing money in 1976, under its trusteeship operation, at the rate of a quarter of a billion dollars annually. Also in 1975-8 millions of dollars in real estate construction loans were in default.

Thus we may not be able to continue believing that the material desires of 215 million people can be satisfied by an economic mechanism whose major fuel is debt.

Depreciating dollars

We may lull ourselves into a sense of security by observing that inflation makes it ever easier and easier to repay money with steadily depreciating dollars. However, inflation also generates high interest rates—the

Increasing Consumer Installment Debt

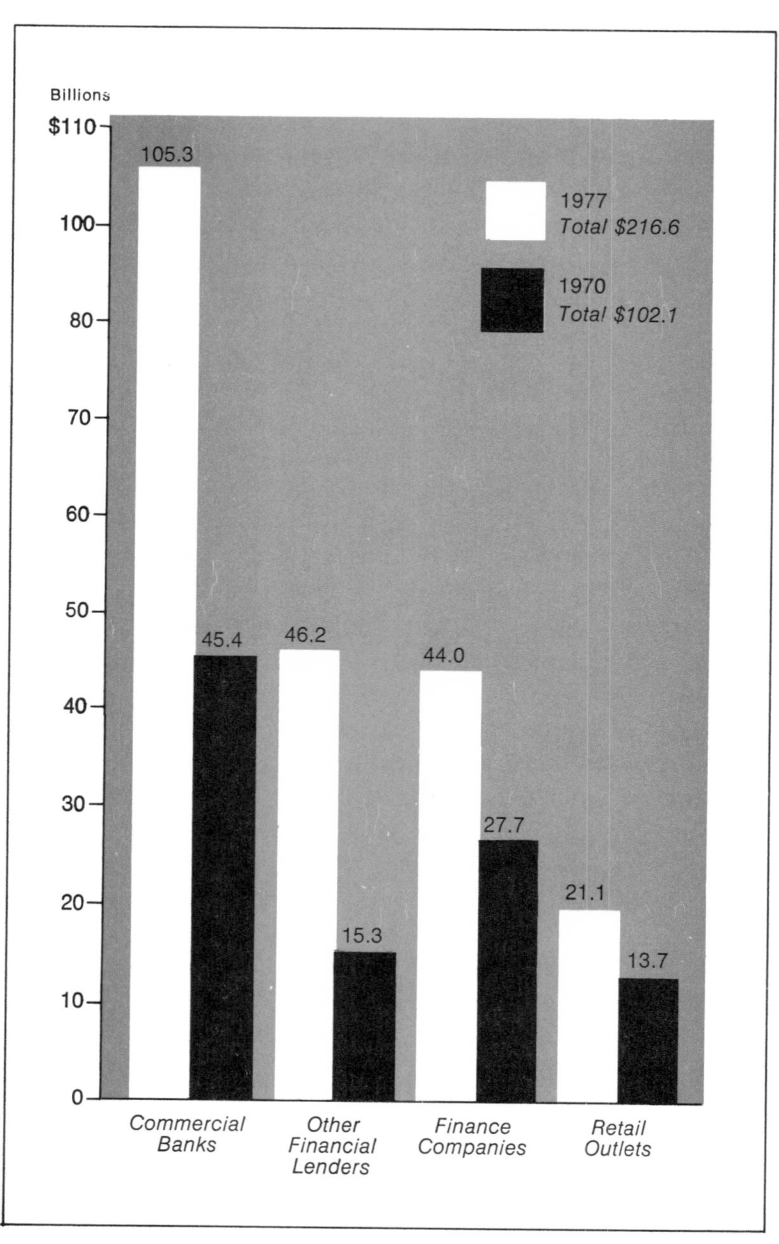

Source: Federal Reserve Board

highest in 100 years in 1974—which can make a big dent in family incomes. Deflation could quite swiftly change the pleasant picture of paying debts with less valuable dollars, and result in financial anguish.

Individuals are already feeling considerable pain. The inflated values of real estate and first-mortgage money, costing 8½ percent, have prevented thousands of young couples from acquiring their own single-family home. The average savings and loan first-mortgage rate in April 1974 was 8¾ percent. The prime rate in June 1974 was 11¾ percent, with the result that those who bought cars or borrowed money on installment contracts at that time have been paying the highest retail interest rates in history. Fortunately, interest rates were lower in 1978.

According to the president of the National Foundation for Consumer Credit, in June 1974 "five or six out of every 100 families were having financial trouble." Middle-income families were feeling the pinch most, probably because their way of life is so solidly built around debt—to acquire a car, a television set, or a boat.

Generally, families manage fairly well if all their monthly interest and payments on debt stay below 20 percent of pretax income. If a family should find that it is exceeding that percentage, there should be an immediate family conference on the subject of debt reduction to devise a plan for reducing purchases.

Whether borrowing rises or falls, it has become indispensable to our way of life. But debt can no longer be entered into lightly or unadvisedly. If you seek "quality of life" and wish to avoid the anxieties and even impaired health which excessive debt may cause, shop prudently for low-interest loans, keep payments well within income flow, and start saying no to some of the temptations offered under the "buy now, pay later" concept.

Glossary

Account—a business relationship in which credit is used.

Actual interest—(see True interest).

Add-on interest—the total interest for the life of the loan, added at the outset to the face amount.

Amortization—the paying off of a debt in regular installments.

Bankruptcy—the state of being unable to pay one's debts. Voluntary, when the initiative is taken by the debtor; involuntary, when certain creditors take the initiative to prevent preferential payments to others.

Budget account—an account in which settlement is made usually in equal monthly payments with an interest charge on the unpaid balance.

Capital gain—the profit realized by the sale of an asset at a price higher than its cost.

Cash value—of life insurance, the amount specified in a policy which an insurance company would pay to the holder if he wished to surrender the policy. Of a motor car, the price the car might be expected to bring if sold at current wholesale price.

Charge account—an account wherein goods or services may be purchased with payment usually due within thirty days of billing.

Collateral—security pledged for the payment of an obligation.

Comaker—a person who, together with the maker, signs a note or a purchase contract and is jointly responsible for its payment.

Commercial bank—a bank providing deposit facilities for checking and savings accounts, loans of money at interest, money exchange facilities, and frequently trust management.

Common stock—a pro-rata share in the earnings, assets, and voting power of a corporation.

Conditional sales agreement—a contract that gives the seller the right to repossess the item sold if the buyer defaults on payments.

Consolidation loan—a loan to combine debts already incurred and to permit systematic reduction of indebtedness by means of one monthly payment to a single creditor.

Convertible—a security exchangeable for another class of security in the same company.

Credit—the providing of funds or the use of funds under an agreement calling for repayment at a future date.

Credit life insurance—life insurance on the borrower for the duration of a loan, decreasing in amount as the loan is repaid.

Credit union—an association of individuals with the purpose of lending money to each other as the need arises.

Deposit—money placed in a bank, a savings and loan association, or a credit union, or a down payment made at the time of a purchase.

Discount interest—the total amount of interest charged for the repayment period which is deducted in advance from a loan, so that the money actually received by the borrower is less than the amount of the loan.

Endorser—a person who affixes his signature to a note or a purchase contract and is responsible for payment if the maker defaults.

Factor—an organization that specializes in certain kinds of loans, principally secured by accounts receivable, inventory, merchandise, machinery, and, less frequently, by securities or real estate.

Finance company—a company which either lends money or provides credit needed for the purchase of goods or services under installment payment contracts.

Foreclose—to convert assets pledged by a debtor to ownership by a creditor; used generally with respect to mortgages in default.

Foreclosure—the act of foreclosing.

Industrial bank—a bank that offers checking and deposit (but no trust) facilities and specializes in amortized personal and industrial loans.

Interest—the charge for the use of money; the rental price of money.

Lien—the claim of a creditor against property of a debtor to assure the payment of a debt.

Line of credit—the amount (often the maximum amount) of credit extended to an individual, company, or partnership.

Listed stock—a stock traded on a stock exchange (most commonly referring to issues on the New York Stock Exchange).

Loan—an advance or extension of money or credit with the expectation of repayment.

Loan shark—an unscrupulous lender of money at usurious rates.

Maker—a person who signs a note or a purchase contract and is directly responsible for its payment.

Mortgage—a loan or claim secured by real estate.

Mutual savings bank—a bank for time deposit (non-checking) accounts entirely owned by its depositors.

Open account—an account in which goods may be charged without any specified maximum dollar limit.

Open-end mortgage—a mortgage that can be restored to its original face amount after it has been reduced by amortization.

Over-the-counter market—the market in all securities not traded on an exchange (and sometimes the trading area for listed issues in large blocks).

Personal finance company (often called personal loan company or small-loan company)—a company that lends money to individuals in limited amounts.

Personal loan—a loan made by an individual.

Personal loan company—(see Personal finance company).

Point—in the arrangement for a home mortgage, a point is 1 percent of the loan.

Preferred stock—a share in the assets and profits of a company, limited to a certain principal amount and a specified dividend return.

Protest—a legal notice that an evidence of indebtedness has been presented for payment and payment has been refused.

Rediscount rate—the annual rate of interest charged by a central bank on loans made to its member banks.

Revolving account—an account in which items may be charged up to a specified dollar limit indefinitely, with payments made by the customer at any time and in any amount, but with interest charged at a monthly rate on the unpaid balance.

Sales finance company—a company that provides credit for purchase of goods and services.

Savings and loan association—a thrift institution that pays interest to depositors and invests its funds principally in real estate mortgages.

Savings bank—a bank which specializes in time deposit accounts, pays regular interest to depositors, and invests its funds in real estate mortgages and bonds.

Second mortgage—a lien that is junior to a first mortgage.

Secured loan—a loan secured by the pledge of property.

Signature loan—a loan secured only by the signature of the maker and possibly comaker.

Simple interest—(see True interest).

Small-loan company—(see Personal finance company).

Stock—the ownership of an equity in a corporation.

True interest (often called actual or simple interest)—the rate, as a percentage of a fixed principal amount, charged for the use of that sum of money for a full year.

Usury—the charging of an excessive, or illegal, rate of interest.

Appendix I

Where to Borrow for Specific Purposes

Where to Get Personal Cash Loans

1. Commercial Bank
2. Credit Union
3. Small-Loan Company
4. Savings Bank (loans against savings account)
5. Savings and Loan Association (loans against savings account)
6. Life Insurance Company (against cash values of policies)
7. Pawnbroker
8. Friends or Relatives
9. Private Lenders (who are sometimes loan sharks)
10. Certain Credit Cards

Where to Get Credit for Purchase of Consumer Goods or Services

1. Store Charge Accounts and Revolving Credit Accounts
2. Restaurant, Hotel, Motel, Gasoline, Telephone, Car Rental Credit Cards
3. All-purpose Credit Cards (American Express, Diners Club, Carte Blanche)
4. Bank Credit Cards (Visa, Master Charge)
5. Commercial Bank
6. Credit Union
7. Finance Company

Where to Get Credit for Purchase of a Car

1. Commercial Bank
2. Finance Company
3. Automobile Dealer
4. Credit Union

Where to Finance Home Ownership by a Mortgage

1. Savings and Loan Association
2. Savings Bank
3. Commercial Bank
4. Life Insurance Company
5. Credit Union
6. Private Mortgage Lender
7. Pension Fund

Where to Get Credit for Home Improvements

1. Commercial Bank
2. Savings Bank
3. Savings and Loan Association
4. Credit Union
5. Finance Company
6. Personal Loan Company

Where to Borrow for Education

1. College or University Student Aid Funds
2. The Tuition Plan, Inc.
3. Commercial Bank
4. Professional Associations
5. Alumni or Fraternity Associations
6. Government-Guaranteed State, Bank, or Educational Institution Loans
7. University Loans to Parents

Where to Get Credit for Purchase of Securities

1. Brokerage Firm (margin account)
2. Commercial Bank

Appendix II

Legal Limits on Interest and Loans by Personal Finance Companies

(By States, July 1977)

Most small-loan laws permit higher interest rates on smaller loans, and many states have several brackets of amounts and charges. The second column of the following table shows two dollar figures: the largest amount to which the highest interest rate may be applied (e.g., $200 in Alabama); and the maximum size of loan permitted (e.g., $300 in Alabama). The third column shows the approximate highest annual percentage rate permitted on the smallest loan (e.g., 36 percent on loans to $200 in Alabama). Interest rates for larger loans are lower than the maximums shown for each state, with the exception of Vermont.

State	*Legal Loan Limits*	*Maximum Annual Percentage Rate*	*Maximum Months Until Maturity*
Alabama	\$200 - \$300	36%	25
Alaska	\$400 - \$1,500	36	none
Arizona	\$300 - \$2,500	36	36½ above \$1,000
Arkansas	No operative law		
California	\$225 - \$10,000	30	84½ above \$6,000
Colorado	\$300 - \$25,000	36	none above \$1,000
Connecticut	\$300 - \$5,000	30	72½ above \$1,800
Delaware	\$1,500 - open	24	84 above \$5,000
Florida	\$300 - \$2,500	30	36½ above \$600
Georgia	\$100 - \$3,000	60	36½
Hawaii	\$100 - \$300	42	20
Idaho	\$480 - \$40,000	36	none above \$1,600
Illinois	\$300 - \$1,500	30	none
Indiana	\$330 - \$32,500	36	none above \$1,300
Iowa	\$250 - \$1,000	36	37 above \$300
Kansas	\$300 - \$25,000	36	37 (\$300-\$1,000)
Kentucky	\$500 - \$1,500	36	36½
Louisiana	\$800 - \$25,000	36	none
Maine	\$480 - \$40,000	30	37 (\$480-\$1,600)
Maryland	\$300 - \$6,000	33	72½ above \$2,000
Massachusetts	\$200 - \$3,000	30	none
Michigan	\$400 - \$1,500	30	none
Minnesota	\$300 - \$1,200	33	36½
Mississippi	\$600 - no max.	36	none
Missouri	\$500 - no max.	27	none
Montana	\$300 - \$7,500	35	none above \$2,500
Nebraska	\$300 - \$3,000	30	36

State	*Legal Loan Limits*	*Maximum Annual Percentage Rate*	*Maximum Months Until Maturity*
Nevada	$300 - $10,000	36	84½ above $7,500
New Hampshire	$600 - $5,000	24	48 above $1,500
New Jersey	$500 - $2,500	24	36½
New Mexico	$150 - $2,500	36	none
New York	$100 - $2,500	30	48½ above $1,400
North Carolina	$300 - $1,500	36	37 above $600
North Dakota	$250 - $1,000	30	24½
Ohio	$750 - $3,000	28	49½ above $1,000
Oklahoma	$300 - $25,000	30	none above $1,000
Oregon	$300 - $50,000	36	none
Pennsylvania	$5,000	27	60½
Rhode Island	$300 - $2,500	36	37 above $1,000
South Carolina	$100 - $7,500	61	60½ above $2,000
South Dakota	$300 - $5,000	30	60½ above $2,500
Tennessee	$100 - open	57	36
Texas	$300 - $2,500	32	43 above $1,500
Utah	$480 - $40,000	36	none above $1,300
Vermont	$1,500	25	36½
Virginia	$500 - $1,500	30	42½ above $1,000
Washington	$500 - $2,500	30	25½
West Virginia	$200 - $1,200	36	36½ above $300
Wisconsin	$1,000 - no max.	23	none above $3,000
Wyoming	$300 - $25,000	36	none above $1,000
Others:			
District of Columbia	No operative law		
Puerto Rico	$300 - $600	35	none
Canada	$300 - $1,500	24	30 above $500

Source: National Consumer Finance Association

Index

Illustrations by Lou W. Skidmore/Spectrum Graphics